the Lives our
mothers
Leave us

Also by Patti Davis

The Long Goodbye

Two Cats and the Woman They Own

❁ ❁ ❁

Hay House Titles of Related Interest

***YOU CAN HEAL YOUR LIFE*, the movie,**
starring Louise L. Hay & Friends
(available as a 1-DVD program and an expanded 2-DVD set)
Watch the trailer at: **www.LouiseHayMovie.com**

***THE SHIFT*, the movie,**
starring Dr. Wayne W. Dyer
(available as a 1-DVD program and an expanded 2-DVD set)
Watch the trailer at: **www.DyerMovie.com**

❁ ❁ ❁

The Age of Miracles: Embracing the New Midlife,
by Marianne Williamson

Dr. Christiane Northrup's Mother-Daughter Wisdom (DVD)

Empowering Women:
Every Woman's Guide to Successful Living, by Louise L. Hay

Healing Your Family History:
5 Steps to Break Free of Destructive Patterns,
by Rebecca Linder Hintze

Naked Babies,
by Nick Kelsh & Anna Quindlen

I'm Still Hungry: *Finding Myself Through Thick and Thin,*
by Carnie Wilson, with Cindy Pearlman

What They Know about Parenting:
Celebrity Moms and Dads Give Us Their Take on Having Kids.
Interviews by Cindy Pearlman; edited by Jill Kramer

❁ ❁ ❁

All of the above are available at your local bookstore, or may be ordered by visiting:
Hay House USA: **www.hayhouse.com**®; Hay House Australia: **www.hayhouse.com.au;**
Hay House UK: **www.hayhouse.co.uk;** Hay House South Africa:
www.hayhouse.co.za; Hay House India: **www.hayhouse.co.in**

THE LIVES OUR
MOTHERS
Leave US

Prominent Women Discuss

the Complex, Humorous, and Ultimately Loving

Relationships They Have with Their Mothers

PATTI DAVIS

HAY HOUSE, INC.
Carlsbad, California • New York City
London • Sydney • Johannesburg
Vancouver • Hong Kong • New Delhi

Published and distributed in the United States by: Hay House, Inc.: www. hayhouse.com • *Published and distributed in Australia by:* Hay House Australia Pty. Ltd.: www.hayhouse.com.au • *Published and distributed in the United Kingdom by:* Hay House UK, Ltd.: www.hayhouse.co.uk • *Published and distributed in the Republic of South Africa by:* Hay House SA (Pty), Ltd.: www.hayhouse.co.za • *Distributed in Canada by:* Raincoast: www.raincoast.com • *Published in India by:* Hay House Publishers India: www.hayhouse.co.in

Editorial supervision: Jill Kramer • *Design:* Amy Gingery

Library of Congress Cataloging-in-Publication Data

Davis, Patti.
  The lives our mothers leave us : prominent women discuss the complex, humorous, and ultimately loving relationships they have with their mothers / Patti Davis.
     p. cm.
  ISBN 978-1-4019-2162-0 (tradepaper : alk. paper) 1. Parents of celebrities--United States. 2. Mothers--United States. 3. Mothers and daughters--United States. 4. Celebrities--United States. I. Title.
  HQ755.8.D377 2009
  306.874'3092273--dc22   2008031911

ISBN: 978-1-4019-2162-0

12 11 10 09 4 3 2 1
1st edition, April 2009

Printed in the United States of America

"WHAT PARENTS LEAVE YOU
IS THEIR LIVES."

— Frank Bidart, from "Lament for the Makers"

contents

INtRODUCtION

ometime around the age of 40, most of us realize that our mothers live deep inside us and always will. It isn't an accident that everyone whose story is told in this book is at least that age—it was pretty much my only rule for asking women to participate. Maybe it's some kind of biorhythm; maybe it's hormonal; maybe it's just a point in life when we pause long enough to say, *Okay, I get it now*. Who knows? But 40 seems to be a pivotal point for understanding how all-encompassing the mother/daughter relationship is.

Even if our mothers are gone, they are never gone from us. If we search our internal landscapes, we find them—sometimes etched as delicately as a watermark, sometimes as deep as an engraving. Our mothers stand behind us at the mirror, trail our footsteps, tap on our shoulders. If you burrow under the surface of any woman, you will find what her mother thought about her.

The women featured in this book are all well known for their accomplishments, their art, their trail blazing. Yet when they talk about their mothers, they are simply daughters. Each story is unique and personal, but all are rooted in the awareness of how tied we are to our mothers' hearts—the beating rhythm that first defined our lives when we floated inside their bodies.

Some women have already seen that death doesn't end the relationship. Others are watching the passage of time in their mothers' eyes, in movements that are slower, in shoulders that aren't as straight as they once were.

Those of us on that side wonder how long we have. But then we remind ourselves that we already know the answer—we have forever.

→»«←

Harry Benson

Patti [right] with her mother, Nancy

patti davis

Patti Davis published her first novel in 1982. She is the author of seven books, both fiction and nonfiction. Her most recent books were *The Long Goodbye* and *Two Cats and The Woman They Own*. She has written for many magazines, including *Time, Newsweek, Ladies' Home Journal, Glamour, More,* and *Sunset.*

☻ ☻ ☻

On a bright blue January day, after the taillights of my mother's car had disappeared down her driveway, I walked through the empty house she'd left behind and acquainted myself with her absence. I'd never been there alone before (although I wasn't entirely alone—my new puppy trotted along behind me). It was unexpected, this solitary exploration. She had just been driven away to travel back East for Gerald Ford's funeral service, and the housekeeper hadn't yet arrived. Secret Service agents are always there, but in a separate area, so the hush of the house and what it could teach me was all mine. I walked back across the threshold like a pilgrim about to undertake a journey.

This is not the house I grew up in; it's the one my parents moved to after the White House years—the house they thought would be home to the winding down of their lives together. And it has been . . . just not in the ways they expected.

My father sank into Alzheimer's here. Eventually, the only room he knew was the one that had once been his study and had been transformed into what we simply called "his room" . . . with a hospital bed, an armchair, a small television set for whichever nurse was on duty, and a table full of medical paraphernalia. He died in that room. Our last good-byes still linger like cobwebs in the corners—light as gossamer, strong as wire. For months afterward I would whisper, "Hi, Dad," every time I passed the doorway. It's now been turned back into a study. My mother sits at his desk and answers mail, with photographs of him all around her.

I still feel my father here, but the house is full of my mother. Her careful, precise decorating—small Limoges boxes arranged in concentric circles on an antique mahogany table, vases of artistically arranged flowers, polished silver picture frames containing images of another time. A large oil painting of a sad-eyed man is as familiar as a family member. He watched me from above the fireplace in my childhood home, and he watches me now from above the fireplace in the den. One wall in this room is lined with books, many of them old and rare, leather spines cracked and worn. Their pages haven't been turned in years. The house smells like my mother—the Kiehl's bath oil she likes to soak in and the mysterious scent that every individual has. Houses hold on to people's scents for a long time; I wondered how possessive this house would be of hers.

I walked from room to room, trying to memorize and absorb the feeling of her not being there. When one parent has died and the other is in her 80s, absence has a different weight to it. It feels like a glimpse into the future, and it invites you to study it . . . and study it well.

The house will be empty one day. This is what it will feel like, sound like, I told myself. I walked so slowly that my dog began running in circles around me, confused by my snail's pace. I didn't want to miss anything. I wanted the quiet and the emptiness to seep into me; I wanted every floating memory to stop me in my tracks.

The living room is rarely used these days. The couch and matching armchairs are tightly slip-covered in floral fabric; I searched my memory for how old they are. *Old* was all I could come up with. I can't remember when they weren't there. When I lived in New York and my mother visited my apartment, she was baffled by my loose "Shabby Chic" slipcovers. (It was years ago, at the very beginning of the phenomenon.)

"Those slipcovers don't fit," she said, mildly horrified.

"They're meant to not fit," I explained. "The style is called Shabby Chic, and everything is loose and slouchy. . . ."

"But they don't fit," she insisted.

Months later I was with her in California at a Malibu house that friends of hers were renting. There on the coffee table was Rachel Ashwell's first book, simply titled Shabby Chic.

"Oh, Patti has some of this furniture!" she exclaimed delightedly, apparently thrilled that I wasn't really the style flunky she'd judged me to be.

I've teased her about this, and she's laughed at the memory, acknowledging that, yes, we do have different styles of decorating and she had been a bit quick to judge. Every once in a while, she's asked me if I'd like a particular piece of furniture to be passed down to me; wisely, she's never offered to leave me the living-room couch.

My mother's bedroom has, sadly, been hers alone for years now. The room on the other side of the wall became my father's when a hospital bed and round-the-clock nurses became necessary. She had the king-size bed removed and a queen-size one brought in, hoping to feel less of his absence in the bed they'd shared for nearly 50 years.

But she still sleeps on her side of the bed. The side that was always my father's is smooth and unwrinkled—not even a dent in the pillow. When I was a child, I'd tumble into their bedroom on laundry day, when bedclothes were piled on the floor, and I'd be able to tell which pillow was my mother's and which my father's by the scent they'd left behind. Now there is only my mother's.

In her dressing room, two robes hang neatly on hangers on the back of the door. I know she has probably half a dozen others in her closet. My mother loves robes—or, generationally speaking, perhaps I should say "dressing gowns." I suddenly have an image of her in our old house, decades ago, pregnant with my younger brother, Ron:

She's standing at the screen door that leads to the backyard, and she's wearing a long pink robe. She has basically been confined to bed for the first trimester so she won't miscarry, and she wears that pink robe a lot, the sash loosely tied over the bump that will become my brother. She's smiling at me as I go back and forth on the swing set, my feet aiming for the sky.

❀❀❀

I don't know how long I walked through the empty rooms. Probably not long, but it felt like I was traveling through space, backward and forward between the past and the future. The house was still, hushed as a church, and it was asking me to give it that same reverence.

By breathing into my mother's absence, I knew I was also inhaling her presence—a presence that would never die, not even when she does.

Our mothers slip between our heartbeats. They live in our wombs, our blood, the reflections we see in the mirror. When we're younger, we think they'll move farther away from us; when we're older, we know they never can.

I imagined my mother long before I was able to really know her. When I was a child, I imagined having long, easy, freewheeling conversations with her, the sort of talks friends might have in late-afternoon sunlight over cups of tea.

The reality was far different. I tried her patience, and she intimidated me. More than that, she was one half of a starlit relationship that seemed to exist in its own galaxy. My parents were fused together—hearts, souls, minds. They loved us—my younger brother and me—but when they looked at each other, the rest of the world fell away. The years of tension with my mother that piled up between us like bricks in a wall are well known. Occasionally, even a stranger will say something to me like, "It's great that you and your mother are getting along now." It's almost always a woman who says this, her own story simmering in her eyes.

As daughters, we bounce off our mothers in ways that are both mysterious and ancient. Even in anger—maybe especially then—we're tethered to them. My mother and I have never been mild with one another. Whether we were miles apart and blaming each other or strongly and lovingly bonded together, our emotions burned up the color chart. Nothing was ever gray.

We do have a friendship now—not that dissimilar to the one I imagined so long ago. But it's been hard-won. At some point, I stopped looking back at the journey and just enjoyed where we've ended up. Apparently, so did she. One day on the phone she said, "I just don't really think about those years anymore." (I think I'd made a passing reference to what I call our "war years.")

❧❧❧

The sound of a car pulling into the driveway made me realize that my pilgrimage through the empty house was over. As I went into the entryway to open the front door, I remembered standing there with my mother two days before my father died. I was on my way out, and she broke down and wept in my arms. My mother is tiny, and I tower over her; her tears streamed down my shoulder and caught in the crook of my arm. "Nothing is ever going to be okay without him," she sobbed.

It's startling and heartbreaking to feel how small our mothers are—to wrap our younger, stronger arms around them and memorize the fragility of their spines beneath our fingers, the softness of their muscles under the weight of our hands. I was holding on to time slipping away; I was holding on to a lifetime of memories, feeling her weep with a sorrow that would never truly heal. I was holding on to the woman who had given birth to me and who was losing the love of her life. But I was finding more of the daughter I wanted to be; and in the end, that's the best we can do.

The Barbara Bush Pearls

The credenza in the entryway of my parents' house is something I immediately check out each time I walk through the door. My mother leaves things there for me, or for others, and occasionally items are just placed there so she won't forget them the next time she goes out—a watch in need of repair or a broken picture frame. I go to her house every Sunday for lunch, and she always leaves the *New York Times Book Review* for me on the silver tray that graces the credenza. Sometimes there are letters for me that people have sent to the Reagan Library.

One Sunday, there was a necklace of large, fake-looking pearls on top of the *New York Times Book Review*. They almost looked like the pop beads I played with as a kid. There's no other way to say it—they were Barbara Bush pearls, and I couldn't picture my mother wearing them.

So, imagine my surprise when she asked, "Would you like these pearls? They're not real. But do you want them?"

"Uh . . . no thanks," I answered, feeling suddenly worried about her mental state. Did she really think I would want those?

Her expression darkened; tension moved into the room. I was, to say the least, confused. "Well, why don't you want them?" she asked.

"They're not really my style," I pointed out.

"I just don't know what your style is," she fumed. "How am I supposed to leave you my jewelry when I die if I don't even know what your style is?"

Now I was really confused. Trying to defuse the situation, I rambled on about jewelry that is meaningful to her, most of which my father gave her, which of course

I *would* want. Jewelry can always be redesigned, I said. Besides, hadn't she said the pearls were fake?

Nothing really got resolved. I left after lunch, still confused, and the next day on the phone I apologized for not taking the gift she'd offered and commented that I had clearly done something wrong.

Calmer than the day before, she said, "It's just that I'd been thinking about leaving you my jewelry, and then you said that the necklace wasn't your style . . . it just made me think about the whole jewelry issue."

"But, see, I didn't know there *was* a jewelry issue," I answered.

Beneath the unfolding of that uncomfortable situation was our history together. My mother and I never learned early on to communicate with each other. In fact, we only learned how in the last decade. We don't have a strong foundation beneath our relationship; we have splintered years of resentment and blame and distance. That's just the reality.

The Barbara Bush pearls simply highlighted that. But I think, especially with family relationships, that it's important to start at the point where you are and move on from there. You can't play catch-up. If the goal is peace of mind, there is no peace of mind in trying to shore up the past.

There will probably be more glitches between my mother and me, when we each struggle to figure out how to communicate. But it only matters that we try. I hope the Barbara Bush pearls found a good home, and I'm grateful to them for providing an important lesson.

➤➤➤ ◀◀◀

Carolyn [right] with her mother, Kate

carolyn see

Carolyn See is the author of many novels, including *The Handyman* and *Golden Days,* as well as nonfiction works such as *Making a Literary Life.* She is a book reviewer for the *Washington Post* and has been on the boards of the National Book Critics Circle and PEN/West International. She has won both Guggenheim and Getty fellowships and currently teaches English at UCLA.

❧ ❧ ❧

arolyn See places a small framed photograph in front of me as a prelude to talking about her mother. Daughter and mother are posed but not smiling. Carolyn, who looks to be about eight or nine in the photo, is blonde and tender. Her eyes reach, ask; they are full of a child's eagerness. Her mother has short, severely styled hair, with a tight curl lying flat against her forehead. Her eyes hold back, hold on, dare. I've been friends with Carolyn for a while and knew her mother was, euphemistically speaking, "difficult." But . . .

"She was mean," Carolyn says evenly and matter-of-factly. "She was meaner than mean. She was an alcoholic; she kicked me out at 16 and later threw my sister, Maureen, out, also at 16."

❄ ❄ ❄

Kate Louise Sullivan married George Laws when she was in her early 20s. They told Carolyn often how much they had wanted a child, she being that child. When their marriage unraveled, Kate would have another daughter with her second husband—Maureen, who was born 15 years later.

Tragically, Maureen became addicted to heroin after she left home and eventually died from the ravages of her addiction. Does Carolyn blame her mother for her sister's death?

"Absolutely. That's a no-brainer. I got out and lived with my father, but Maureen was there on her own with our mother, and she went through hell."

She tells me about one incident when Maureen dove beneath the bed to avoid being beaten with a wooden hanger Kate was wielding. "Mother knelt down at the bed, trying to prod her out with the hanger, all the while saying, 'Come on, I won't hurt you.' The thing was, she delighted in her meanness."

❀❀❀

How does a daughter come to terms with a mother who couldn't show love to her children? Carolyn readily credits therapy, as well as some of the '80s self-help programs that preached dealing with your own "self-dramas"—in other words, hold on to the pain and you're choosing to do so. But therapy only works if it leads to understanding . . . if it leads to looking back down the years of your parents' lives to see where the ground cracked beneath them, where the fissures opened. It's a strange kind of topographical study. When did the landscape shift? When did the heart roll down a dark ravine and get lost?

❂❂❂

Kate grew up as the caretaker for her own mother, who was ill and dying from tuberculosis. At 11 years old, she was changing bedsheets, sponging off her mother's body, cleaning up the sputum and the blood, and waiting for death to roll in.

One day Kate's older brother stood over their ailing mother and demanded money; when she said she didn't have any, he hit her across the face. Kate got on her bike, rode to her father's workplace, and told him what had happened. "Well, what do you want me to do about it?" he snapped.

Not a great foundation for motherhood later on.

Carolyn was born in 1934 in Pasadena, California, in the midst of America's Great Depression. She was born to two people who carried their own war-torn histories with them. Her father's mother "blew her brains out" when he was 14, and he was the one who found her body.

Carolyn learned over the years that by tracing the map of her mother's history, she could start drawing her own . . . to peace of mind for herself. She could eventually accept, as she says now, that her mother was ill, that she couldn't have behaved any differently even if she'd wanted to.

"It wasn't so bad for the first 11 years," she concedes. "We lived in Eagle Rock then—a small town. But when I was 11, my father left her, and us. Just walked out very cavalierly. I think that really let loose her rage."

At 16, Carolyn went to live with her father and his new wife in a one-room apartment in Los Angeles. She was happy with him, but her mother's fury was not forgotten, or absent from her life. Kate had gotten remarried—to a fellow alcoholic who thought he could get away with abusing her. Carolyn laughs and points out the importance of finding humor in even the grimmest stories. "He didn't know what he was getting himself into," she says. "He didn't know what mean was. He had definitely met his match."

There was no humor, though, in her sister Maureen's circumstances. Where Carolyn was stubborn and stoic, Maureen was terrified. She was also wily enough to try to escape her mother's brutality. One night Kate and a female friend nailed plywood over the window Maureen had tried to crawl out of. They held her down and smashed her head into the floor again and again. Not surprisingly, when Maureen finally did leave at 16, she ran into the arms of heroin.

Anyone would understand if Carolyn had banished her mother from her life. Especially when she had her own children: two daughters and later a stepdaughter. Who *wouldn't* nod their head and say yes if the story whittled down to exile—to a mother and daughter locked out from each other's lives with distance and silence? But that's not the turn the story took.

Carolyn's daughters knew their grandmother and even have their own stories about her. But they also learned how humor lifts up even the darkest veils of one's history. They now joke about "channeling Grandma Kate" whenever one of them has a temper tantrum. And they know of what they speak. One Christmas, Carolyn and the man she was seeing, along with her daughters and her mother, stayed in a woodsy California cabin for the holiday. Carolyn's daughter Clara, who was four at the time, put out cookies and milk for Santa and asked her grandmother if she thought he would like them.

Kate, drunk and characteristically brutal, snarled, "There is no Santa Claus."

It was Clara who, years later, would drive Carolyn to Kate's bedside as she lay dying. It was Clara who, after her grandmother was once again predictably unkind even on her deathbed, started laughing on the way home in response to Carolyn's question: "Do you think she was happy we came?"

We teach what we've learned over the years. Carolyn has raised three daughters who have learned to look at meanness through the filter of humor. They know their own mother's history—they've lived part of it—but most of all, they've seen what she did with it. That's where the alchemy comes in, and ultimately the victory. We can't choose our family history; we can only choose how we react to it.

"I feel sad for my mother," Carolyn says. "I pity her. She was ill. Expecting her to be different would have been like asking a frog to learn Latin."

And as easily as she can talk about the horrors, she can talk about the positives.

"Let me tell you the good things about my mother: She was wonderful to her friends—loyal, supportive. She was the one who would take a friend to the hospital, sit with them, care for them. She kept a lovely house; she was a great gardener. If I look around my home, even though my taste isn't identical to hers, I can see how I really channeled her sense of style. And even the anger—there have been times in my life, professionally, when being able to pull out some anger in myself and use it in a particular way came in very handy."

There also came a moment in Carolyn's professional life when that anger was aimed straight at her mother. Carolyn and John Espey, her "life partner" of 26 years who died in September 2000, were giving a lecture in San Bernardino. Unbeknownst to them, Kate was in the audience. At the conclusion of the lecture when Carolyn and John were signing autographs, Kate approached them and made her presence known. Then she said to the people gathered around, "I used to beat her up pretty good. I guess I'd get arrested for that now."

As Carolyn tells it, she went home from that encounter and "went berserk." Of all the unforgivable things her mother had done, this one moved up to the front of the line. "She brought one world into the other," Carolyn says. "She crashed into my professional life, and I was furious."

Yet still, when she got the news that her mother was ill and probably dying, she went to her bedside. In the end, that says everything. It's possible that in families, we are more haunted by the things we don't do than by the words we've said or the deeds we come to regret. Her mother was dying, and Carolyn drove miles to be there; it's the best way to put ghosts to rest—by just showing up.

One of the most profound moments Carolyn recounts happened when John was ill and bedridden. Carolyn was his primary caregiver. She changed bedsheets, she kept him clean . . . she stepped into the role her mother had known at the young age of 11. And she says there was a moment when she truly understood how that part of her mother's background had shaped her—the profound exhaustion; the frustration; the weight of caring for a dying person day after day, night after night. Carolyn was wise enough to find time for grief, but maybe Kate never did, never could. She was, after all, only a child.

And who knows where all that sadness goes if you don't get a chance to express it?

Carolyn See took the raw material of an angry and unloving mother and turned it into a full, rich life for herself. She did it by working hard for understanding and, ultimately, acceptance. She did it by wrapping her heart, her mind, and her humor around the complicated woman who, despite her flaws and her fury, brought a daughter into the world who would figure out how to forgive her.

⇢⇠

Melissa [right] with her mother,
Barbara; and brother, Jonathan

meLissa GiLBeRt

In 1974, **Melissa Gilbert** beat out 500 other young girls for the role of Laura Ingalls Wilder in the TV series *Little House on the Prairie.* The show ran for nine years, and Melissa literally grew up before our eyes. She has continued to work regularly, mainly in television. In 2001, she was elected president of the Screen Actors Guild and served two terms. She is the youngest person ever to receive a star on the Hollywood Walk of Fame.

❀ ❀ ❀

a few days before we got together to talk, Melissa witnessed an exchange between her mother, her younger sister, Sara, and Sara's three-year-old son, Levi.

"Levi had put something in his mouth that didn't belong there, my mother had taken it from him, and he'd started crying."

Melissa sat back and watched as her mother desperately tried to quiet his tears, to distract him from being upset . . . until Sara intervened and said, "Mom, let him have his feelings."

Melissa describes what happened next: "My mother sat down, looking like she was literally in physical pain—because her grandson was crying and no one was letting her stop it. It was a pivotal moment for me. It closed the circle. Because I'd been carrying around a lot of resentment about the fact that I'd never been allowed to grieve or be sad, especially when my father died. I was 11 at the time, and I remember it as this blur—I was hysterical when she told me Daddy had died, but then my brother and I weren't allowed to go to the funeral because she thought it would be too painful for us. Whenever we were sad or angry or sick, my mother would say, 'No, no, no,' and sprinkle fairy dust over everything to try and make us happy again. But the other night, watching her with my nephew, I realized that none of it was done maliciously or selfishly—she just wanted to protect her babies from pain."

❄❄❄

Melissa Gilbert was born on May 8, 1964, and adopted by Paul Gilbert, an actor and comedian; and Barbara Crane, an actress. Her parents actually had arranged the adoption before her birth. Barbara has told Melissa that she stayed by the phone for 24 hours when her birth mother went into labor. Her brother, Jonathan, was adopted three years later.

The desire to "sprinkle fairy dust over everything" made the Gilbert household a magical place in many ways. Barbara hand-made the Halloween costumes for Melissa and Jonathan and turned every holiday into a festive occasion. She helped create imaginative games and stories for her children—a whimsical, make-believe world she probably hoped would keep the real one at bay, with all its sadnesses and challenges. But life slips through even the best-laid plans. So does death.

"February 13th, the day my father died, is still such a hard day for me," Melissa says. "I'm a walking zombie that day, mainly because I didn't get a chance to grieve when it happened. It wasn't until I was in my 20s that I gave myself permission to feel my feelings."

Melissa has two sons—Dakota, from her first marriage to Bo Brinkman; and Michael, with Bruce Boxleitner, to whom she's been married for 13 years.

"Intuitively," she says, "and without deliberately thinking it through, I've raised my kids to express whatever feelings they have. There isn't anything they feel that they aren't encouraged to talk about. When we had to put one of our dogs down, I asked Michael if he wanted to go with us to the vet's office, and he said yes. It was hard, but no harder or easier because he was there. I let him make the choice."

For years, Melissa longed to talk to her mother about the emotions she hadn't been allowed to express as a child, especially those surrounding her father's death. But Barbara still preferred to dance away into happier subjects. At one point, a therapist Melissa was seeing said, "Why do you keep going to the hardware store for bread?"

"I can look now at the bits and pieces I know of how my mother was raised and see how that molded her and shaped her," Melissa says. "My grandmother, who is now 90, was 18 when she got married, 19 when she had my mother. At that age, no one is terribly patient. So I suspect my mother swore she was going to be different from *her* mother." Somewhere along the line, the notion of protecting her children from any kind of upset evolved.

With that agenda guiding her, Barbara found a sweet and unique way of telling her two children that they were adopted. She got a book about "special-chosen children" and crossed out the names of the fictional children, replacing them with Melissa's and Jonathan's names. Melissa believed that the book had actually been written about her and her brother. She recalls going to school and telling a classmate that she was "special-chosen." The child said, "Do you mean adopted?"

"No!" Melissa answered defiantly. "Special-chosen! Adopted children come from orphanages."

When she went home, she told her mother about the exchange, and Barbara gently explained that some people do refer to it as adoption, but that she and Jonathan were absolutely "special-chosen." They were wanted and loved from the start.

Years later when Melissa was in her 20s and wanted to locate her birth parents, Barbara moved past the fear that all adoptive parents have and responded with understanding and support. It turned out that her birth mother had passed away, but Melissa located her birth father in Las Vegas and arranged a visit. Barbara put together a scrapbook for her to give him—snapshots of his daughter's childhood from infancy on through to the present day. But the visit was sadly unfulfilling and disappointing.

"He was very distant, very cut off," Melissa says. "I wanted some emotion from him and got nothing. And then he told me that he thought I was born in 1963 instead of 1964. So, on top of everything that he wasn't giving me that I'd wanted to find there, I left thinking I was a year older than I'd always believed. I called my mother that night, sobbing hysterically. And she talked me down. She was patient and gentle and just talked until I calmed down . . . and she swore that, yes, I was born in 1964—he was wrong about that. I was so upset, and it was really extraordinary how she talked me in off that ledge." Melissa smiles at the memory and adds, "So sometimes you *can* get bread from a hardware store."

❂❂❂

Melissa began working in commercials when she was barely out of diapers, but not because Barbara was a hard-driving stage mother. She had, instead, been influenced by people who commented on how cute and precocious her daughter was and that she would probably be easily cast. Melissa remembers one audition when she was around two.

"I walked into this room; and the director, the producer, the advertising guy, the writer, and the casting director were all sitting around on the floor. It was 1966—that's how they did things then! I walked right over to the director, climbed into his lap, and kissed him on the cheek. My mother was terrified they were going to think she'd made me do that, but she hadn't. It was all me."

Barbara put strict rules on Melissa's schedule, not allowing her to work more than a day or two every week . . . that is, until the age of nine when she was cast in *Little House on the Prairie.* When she talks about loved ones and parental figures, Michael Landon, who played her father on the show, is included. "My mother is the only one left now in terms of parents," she says. "My father and my grandfather are gone. Michael Landon, who was my mentor and like a father to me, is gone. . . ."

Barbara has been married several times—a challenging thing for Melissa to get her head around. Her own marriage to Bruce has endured and deepened over the years because they've committed themselves to working on it, even going to therapy together during rough patches. But she's accepted that, in this area, she and her mother are different.

"I can see in myself parts of my mother and parts of my grandmother, but they're the best parts of them. Those are the parts I've chosen to take on. What I look for now when I'm with my mother is whatever will bring me peace of mind. I don't need to explain my relationship with Bruce or pursue conversations that are difficult for her to have with me or look for things from her that she isn't able to give."

❄❄❄

Melissa told me all of this before life turned—the way it tends to do—and her mother's husband, Warren Cowan, passed away. Sometimes we learn a lot about our mothers by stepping bravely into their world—often into shadowy rooms where death is moving in.

"I just watched my mother take care of Warren the last month of his life," Melissa told me, months after we first spoke. "Then I watched him die in her arms. Literally, I was standing there watching her in bed with him, holding his head to her breast as he died. I didn't realize the depth of their love story until then. Seeing that defined the word *beauty* for me."

Looking at our mothers through different eyes means looking at everything else differently as well, even aspects of our past.

❂❂❂

Throughout her life, Melissa had a second mother figure to come to terms with. Like most adopted children, she went through a stage of wondering why her birth mother had given her up. Was she not loved or lovable? Was she not wanted? Then she learned that her birth parents had brought six children into the world between them—she was number seven. There simply wasn't enough money to support another child.

"I think my birth mother had such courage and showed such love for me, giving me up and allowing me to have a better life than she could have provided," Melissa says. "I can't imagine how difficult it would be to give up a child, and I'm so grateful to her that she had that strength, that she loved me so much."

She has a single photograph of her birth mother. It's a small black-and-white picture of a slender woman with thick, wavy black hair. She's sitting on a chair in a clearing out in the woods. She has a cast on one leg from the knee down, and she's dressed in jeans and a jacket. In her hands is a rifle that she's pointing toward the trees.

"You can't see her face," Melissa says, "but you definitely get a sense of her."

Photographs freeze more than time. They immortalize the subject in a specific mood, a specific stance, perhaps with the trail of a passing emotion still in the person's eyes. They also lock the observer into all that was contained in that one moment when the camera clicked. Melissa's birth mother will always be that spunky black-haired woman with a cast on her leg and a rifle in her hands. No other images, no other reality, ever moved in to argue with that.

Melissa had an open field in which to let her heart decide how to process the fact that the woman who brought her into the world then gave her up for adoption. It's possible that if they'd met, both the image in the photograph and a daughter's emotional choices—no less brave than her mother's—might have been challenged.

The visit might have been disappointing, as was the one with her father.

So it might be a little bit of magic that things worked out the way they did. But Melissa believes that she and the woman who gave birth to her will one day meet. "On a spiritual level," she says, "I look forward to the time when I see her on the other side and I can thank her."

❂❂❂

Melissa's journey with Barbara continues to deepen and evolve . . . even in the short time since we first spoke. Witnessing the fierce love her mother had for her husband, the way her arms held him at the end, the way her heart would hold him forever, changed the topography of their relationship.

"I've been with her or spoken with her every day since, and it's been truly phenomenal. It's like someone took off her armor."

But the truth about armor is that we need to drop our own before we can appreciate that someone else has. Death taught both Barbara and Melissa about life—about how to live it differently, at least with each other. And about how to embrace the love that was always there.

"When the time comes for one of us to go—whichever one goes first, because you never really know what will happen in life—neither of us will have to say to the other, 'Did you love me?' or 'Do you love me?' It's never been in doubt. I've never questioned whether my mother loved me—I always knew she did, and I always loved her."

In the end, that's everything. Other questions might remain and never be answered. But for Melissa, the most important one was answered the day she was born.

≫≪

Anna on her mother, Prudence's, lap

aNNa QUINDLeN

Anna Quindlen is a best-selling author of both fiction and nonfiction. Her novels include *Blessings, One True Thing,* and *Object Lessons.* Her nonfiction works include *Living Out Loud, Loud and Clear, Naked Babies* (with Nick Kelsh), and *Good Dog. Stay.* She has also written children's books. Her *New York Times* column "Public & Private" won the Pulitzer Prize in 1992. She has a column in *Newsweek* every other week.

❦ ❦ ❦

"the world might be tired of hearing me talk about my mother," Anna Quindlen told me when I asked her to be part of this book. Not so. She is an eloquent voice in the never-tiresome story of daughters and mothers. It would be hard for me to imagine this book without her contribution.

Anna was 19, the oldest of five children, when her mother, Prudence Quindlen, died of ovarian cancer at the age of 40.

To lose one's mother at a young age is to lose chances, possibilities, and unlit dreams you thought would always be waiting up ahead. It's like suddenly realizing that one of the most vital parts of your future was written across the sky in vapor trails. "I was more or less the primary caregiver," she says. "My father traveled a lot on business, and I dropped out of college to take care of her and my four younger siblings."

Anna's mother kept her illness a secret from most of the family for a year. Only her husband knew that she had been diagnosed with stage IV ovarian cancer. "But," Anna says, "for the last six months she was very sick, going through bouts of chemo and responding little, if at all, to increasingly large doses of morphine."

Some of those doses were administered by Anna—a heartbreaking responsibility for a 19-year-old girl. When I suggest that there might, however, be something tender and haunting in the role reversal of a daughter caring for her mother, Anna says, "Honestly, I wish it had been tender and haunting, but I was a selfish and egocentric teenager, and I was terrified by the idea that I would be trapped in the suburbs caring for my family into perpetuity. I would have done anything at the time to avoid the responsibility. Now, of course, I can only imagine how riven with guilt and self-loathing I would be had I not taken on the task."

In every family, there are trails of footprints left behind over years, decades. Some veer off, circle around and back, and finally—if we're lucky—forge ahead on a path that was always waiting there.

Anna may have been "angry and resentful" at the time—an emotional cover for the fact that she was losing her mother, the most important person in her world—but she grew into the woman who wrote (in *A Short Guide to a Happy Life*):

Something really bad happened to me, something that changed my life in ways that, if I had had a choice, it would never have been changed at all. And what I learned from it is what, today, sometimes seems to be the hardest lesson of all.

I learned to love the journey, not the destination. I learned that this is not a dress rehearsal, and that today is the only guarantee you get.

❦ ❦ ❦

One of the ironies of life is that often the deepest wisdom comes from the cruelest blows. The death of a parent changes you forever. But the loss is fluid, amorphous. It alters its shape, its dimensions, as you move through the years.

Anna got married; had three children; built a career and a solid, happy life—all of it around the gap of her mother's absence. And yet . . . the fact that her daughter bears a strong resemblance to Prudence brings her pure joy. When she thinks about how much her mother loved her, Anna says she feels free of any self-doubt, fortified with confidence. There are, of course, sorrowful moments, too.

Twenty-five years after Prudence Quindlen died, on the anniversary of her death, Anna published an article in *Good Housekeeping* (later reprinted in her collection *Loud and Clear*) in which she wrote:

There's just a hole in my heart, and nothing to plug it. The truth is that there's no one, ever, in your life like your mother. And that's even if she's a bad mother, punitive, critical. Your mother is the mirror. Whether you elect to gaze at the reflection with equanimity, to tilt the glass or crack it outright, it is the point from which you always begin. It is who you are.

It's now been more than 35 years. "I can say without hyperbole," Anna tells me, "that I think of her every day, and I try to be the mother to my own children that she was to hers. She was most remarkable for her kindness and quiet, gentle nature. I was so lucky to have such a decent, honest, warm person as my mother, a woman who had a gift for loving unconditionally."

It could be looked at in this way: a 19-year-old girl was deprived of years, decades even, with her mother. They never got to grow alongside each other. But Anna has proven that this is not the whole story. It's true that there's a grief that never goes away. But even many years after her death, Anna's mother slips into her daughter's life and nestles in quiet, sleepy corners.

"I try every day to wake up and be like her for the sake of my children," Anna has written.

There may be no greater testament to how relationships endure, even over the boundary line of death.

-»»-«««-

Rosanna [left] with her mother, Mardi

ROSANNA ARQUETTE

Rosanna Arquette is a Golden Globe–nominated actress, as well as a director and producer. She began acting as a teenager and has appeared on television as well as in films. She is known for starring in independent films such as *Desperately Seeking Susan,* for which she won a British Academy Award. In 2002, she wrote, produced, and directed the film *Searching for Debra Winger.*

❀ ❀ ❀

Rosanna Arquette almost wasn't born. Her mother, Mardi, was 19, pregnant, and lying on a table waiting for a doctor to perform an abortion. It was 1958— not a friendly era for young girls who weren't ready to become mothers. Suddenly the nurse ran in and told Mardi to get up, get dressed, and get out of there. She did . . . just before the doctor was arrested and hauled off to jail.

"I've wondered," Rosanna says, "if that's lodged in me, that abandonment thing."

Well, it is an unusual start to one's life.

Rosanna is someone who investigates, questions— how does the past snag the present, leak into the future? As a single mother of a 13-year-old daughter, Zoe, she doesn't want to repeat any ancient patterns, especially those that caused damage. She has dedicated herself to working through the remnants of her past in therapy in order to have healthier relationships and be the best mother she can be.

"Everything ultimately gets back to your mother and father," she says. "My mother and I had a very intense relationship. Very violent and tumultuous for the first part of my life.

"My siblings didn't have the same experiences with her that I did. With me, she could be pretty abusive— sometimes physically, but much of the time verbally. She'd just wig out. But the thing was, she realized that about herself. She came from a really violent, crazy home herself; and she didn't have the tools necessary to break the cycle."

So Mardi set out to get those tools. She decided to become a therapist. Already an actress and a poet, she brought that same creative passion to studying and practicing therapy. She focused primarily on treating abused women.

As the oldest of five children, Rosanna watched her mother grow and change. She saw her learn how to be a more patient mother than the girl who'd struggled to raise a baby in the '60s with little money.

"All of us in my family have had the experience over the years of people stopping us and telling us how much our mother helped them as a therapist. Women have told me that she saved their lives."

It takes courage to go back—to look at where you came from, who you came from, and start snipping at threads so you can be free to grow. Mardi taught her firstborn a valuable lesson by her own example, one that was not lost on Rosanna: dare to go back so you can ultimately go forward.

❦❦❦

Although Rosanna's four siblings fared better than she did, none of them had what could even remotely be called a conventional upbringing. No white picket fence and swing set in the yard. From age 11 to 14, Rosanna lived with her family in a commune. Her brother David was born in the back of a van that was taking Mardi from the commune to a hospital. Rosanna remembers that the following day she attended the birth of a boy who would become David's best friend. She was 12 at the time.

Years later, in the '80s, Mardi took her four younger kids to the Diablo Canyon nuclear power plant for a demonstration. They lay down in the road with other antinuclear protesters and refused to move. Mardi was a woman of conviction and was determined to impart that to her children.

"Also," Rosanna says to me, laughing, "when your father cut back federal money for the homeless and there were suddenly more homeless people on the streets, my mother started bringing them home. Another time, she was getting on a bus to go to a protest march and the driver refused to let a crippled man on who was using a walker. She sat down in the street in front of the bus and wouldn't move until the driver let the man get on."

It's not surprising that all of Mardi's children are uniquely creative people. One couldn't imagine a banker emerging from such Bohemian and spontaneous beginnings.

❀❀❀

Rosanna left the commune at 14, moved in with family friends in New Jersey for a year, and then hitchhiked across the country. During the next few years, her family moved to Chicago and later to Los Angeles.

"The funny thing about my mother," Rosanna says, "is that she was this spiritual seeker, but at the same time she was a bit of a stage mother. Both my parents were struggling actors, so when I began working and earning money, they kind of lived vicariously through me."

She recalls one incident when she was older, sitting in a therapy session that her parents were also attending. "It was one of those sessions based on Al-Anon, where each person says how they felt when such and such happened. I was stunned when my mother said, 'We were really hurt when you turned down the lead in *The Accused.'* I realized how emotionally invested they'd been in my career choices."

She can laugh about that now, but it wasn't exactly a source of humor at the time.

Her mother and father also dealt with their own tumultuous relationship. Mardi had managed to create a smoother path with her children, but that didn't always extend to her marriage. The emotional ups and downs were constant, and Rosanna's father wasn't always faithful. It's another tracing from her past that Rosanna wonders about: do we re-create versions of our parents' relationship, hungry for a different outcome?

Her mother would almost certainly want the question to be asked.

☺☺☺

Mardi was diagnosed with breast cancer when Rosanna was 30, and she couldn't bring herself to go in the direction of Western medicine. "She made the decision that felt right to her," Rosanna says. "She didn't have any regrets about her choice."

The cancer spread and worsened. After nearly eight years, her breast turned gangrenous, and no one in the family could afford to be shy about the subject of death—it was closing in. Mardi's children accepted the responsibility of caring for their mother during the last stages of her life.

"My sister Patricia did the hard Florence Nightingale parts," Rosanna tells me. "The cleaning and bandaging, even injections. She was amazing. But we all cared for her together, knowing the best we could do at that point was keep her comfortable." For Rosanna, it was the completion of a circle with Mardi—a tempestuous beginning, followed by years of work on their relationship, and finally the soft willingness of a daughter to care for her mother as she slips away from life.

"I feel really clear with her," Rosanna can say now. "We were in a good place at the end. She got her therapist's license a week before she died. She'd put in all the hours, she'd been counseling people, but she didn't actually get her license until just before she died. It was really important to be able to show that to her."

Mardi died in August, just shy of 59. It was four days before Rosanna's 38th birthday.

"August is a hard month for me. The first year after she died, I went to the cemetery and just sat by her grave most of the day."

She and David were there when their mother took her last breath. Everyone knew the time was near; Mardi had stopped eating. But determining when the end will come for anyone is hardly an exact science. She lingered for a couple of weeks and died early one morning, after Rosanna had spent the night sleeping in Mardi's room.

"David and I were both telling her it was okay to let go. She looked like a fish out of water," Rosanna recalls. "Her eyes were wide and staring, but it was really like she was no longer here, like her soul had already left. It was pretty peaceful, actually. But then I had to call Patricia— that was really hard."

Rosanna's father died a few years later from complications following a blood transfusion. "They'd had their issues, but I think he died really knowing that my mom was his great love."

Rosanna is very clear about how her mother lives inside her.

"She was so creative and so dedicated to standing up for what she believed. Even the way she died—it's how she wanted it. She didn't want surgery or to be pumped full of chemo. There was a lot of integrity in her choices. And she raised five children who are all creative and artistic. She had a full life. She was an actress, a therapist, a poet . . ."

Ten years ago, Rosanna spent most of a warm August day sitting quietly at her mother's grave site. We sit beside the graves of loved ones to listen to the silence they've left behind, but also to explore the lives they've left us with, the lives that lean into our souls, that shape us in both obvious and mysterious ways.

Mardi left Rosanna some memories to work through, it's true, but she left others that sustain her, guide her. And she left her daughter with poetry, including a poem about her:

She Child

Like clockwork
My body follows a tide
Wakes me with bright red ribbons

Asks who sets the sun in the sky.
The first time I lay down with a man
He sprayed branches with semen
Stuck his horn in trunks
Sorry it went so fast he said
Pulling up his pants
Next time I'll give you an orgasm.
What's that I asked he laughed tossing a quarter in the air
Like a gem.
In the summer I did quiver come
Permission given with one I would marry
Grew robust as an apple
Until rough hands put me to sleep like thugs.
Still I must have squeezed my knees
Pushed down hard because she traveled out juicy and ripe
An exquisite immaculate world of sun.
She child in your loving know seasons come and seasons go
And autumn will pull on you
Sure as the moon.
Last week my father staggered on the beach
Said nothing in life is ever complete.
I have sat with a friend until her breath
Stopped counting possibilities
Running out of me like clots
Expect the nesting of one last egg will wash away winter's ebb
While womanhood is a circle of perfect red
Tied in a banner around my head.

➤➤➤ ◄◄◄

Mary Kay [sitting on her mother, Gwendolyn's, lap] with her father and brother

mary kay place

Mary Kay Place is an actress, singer, director, and screenwriter. In 1977, she won an Emmy for her role as Loretta Haggers in *Mary Hartman, Mary Hartman*. She has written scripts for several TV sitcoms and has acted in many films, including *The Rainmaker* and *Being John Malkovich*. She has directed shows for HBO and has a recurring role on the HBO series *Big Love*.

❀ ❀ ❀

When Mary Kay Place says, "It never occurred to me my mother wouldn't be there for me," it's not clear at first if she's referring to the past or the present. Gwendolyn Lucille Place died in 2003 of complications related to Alzheimer's.

With the death of a parent, there is an unfamiliar emptiness—a persistent feeling that he or she is still just a phone call away. But Alzheimer's compounds the ache, because the journey of loss begins years before death has the final word. With every passing month and year, with every visit, the person you once knew has faded some more; all you can do is remember who they once were.

That is probably hovering somewhere behind Mary Kay's comment, but she's actually referring to her childhood. The Place home was lively, warm— occasionally tumultuous, but always grounded in love. Mary Kay is the middle child, the only girl sandwiched between two brothers, and none of them ever doubted that their parents were absolutely devoted to them.

❁❁❁

Gwendolyn Lucille, whom everyone called Gwen, married her college sweetheart in Texas just before World War II. It was a time when many young men said good-bye to their new brides and traveled across the ocean, not knowing if they would return in one piece, or at all. By the time Mary Kay's father joined the Marines and sailed off to fight in the war, Gwen was pregnant with her first child. A war bride living in Port Arthur, Texas, she became a schoolteacher—a career she would set aside once her husband returned from the war, but would take up again when Mary Kay was a sophomore in high school.

"She was a good teacher," Mary Kay says. "She would take kids who caused trouble in other classes and give them special attention. She'd make them class monitor, or somehow show trust and interest in them when no one else had. But then she'd say to them, 'You have to live up to this responsibility. No more bad behavior—I'm counting on you.' When my mom died, we got letters from a lot of her former students. One wrote that my mother inspired her to become a teacher even though she'd spent a lot of recess periods writing 100 times: 'I will not talk in class.'"

By the time Mary Kay was born, the family had moved to Tulsa, Oklahoma, and five years later her younger brother was born. Gwen settled into the life of a typical '50s homemaker; she was a homeroom mother, a Camp Fire leader, a Little League volunteer.

"She was very involved in our lives," Mary Kay says. "We knew we could always count on her, but we also knew that if we got in trouble, we'd have to take responsibility for our actions. She was never one to deny the truth about her children or sugarcoat things. She got that attitude from her parents, who were very pragmatic, pull-yourself-up-by-the-bootstraps people. They didn't believe in feeling sorry for yourself, and neither did my mother. Mainly, it was a matter of choosing to focus on the positive."

Gwen's relationship with her husband was a bit more complicated.

"At first glance, my parents had a traditional postwar marriage. My father was head of the household and a college professor, with a big, outgoing personality and community recognition. He was the star, and Mom was the supporting player. But where it counted, they were equal partners. She always spoke her mind, and since they both had strong personalities, they argued a lot—it was just their way.

"Once when we were kids, the whole family was traveling in the car to my grandparents' home in Texas, and Daddy was in a hurry to get there. He was cranky and kept passing one country diner after another, saying it didn't look right or didn't seem clean enough. Finally, he agreed to stop at some dinky store. Mother went in and bought groceries so we could eat in the car and keep going. While she was struggling to make sandwiches in her lap, Daddy was on a roll—telling her to be careful with the mayo on the car's seat, don't let the tomato drip . . . he was going on and on. Finally she said, 'One more word and I'm throwing this out.'

"Well, he couldn't resist a few more comments; and sure enough, down went the window and out went the bread, the mayonnaise, the potato salad, lettuce, tomatoes—all of it. My brothers and I looked at our lunch on the highway behind us, stunned.

"But Daddy got the point—we stopped at the next restaurant. For my parents, arguing was just blowing off steam, a way to work things out. Flare-ups were over as quickly as they started, and they didn't hold on to any anger. Once it was done, it was as if it had never happened."

We are imprinted as children in many ways, and Mary Kay just assumed that every home was like hers. Later, when she was grown and entering into her own relationships, she found herself following the same pattern she'd grown up with—declaring her feelings, even anger, and expecting the other person to go toe-to-toe with her. She would then expect the whole dustup to be over and forgotten.

Laughing, she says, "Of course it doesn't always work like that. I've definitely freaked out a few people."

Some of the most enduring lessons Mary Kay learned from her mother had to do with empathy and compassion. She recalls coming home one day after school and telling her mother that she'd made plans with a friend but had then gotten a more enticing offer, one that she wanted to take.

"Well, how do you think you'd feel if someone did that to you?" her mother asked. "Put yourself in her shoes."

Another lesson had to do with treating people equally, not making distinctions. Mary Kay didn't know, growing up, that there was such a thing as cattiness between women. She didn't know because her mother had never demonstrated it. Gwen genuinely liked both men and women, never gossiping or talking behind anyone's back. As quaint as it seems, Gwen would tell her children with complete earnestness, "If you can't say something nice, don't say anything at all."

"She wasn't a saint, though," Mary Kay points out. "She could be dogmatic, bossy, and stubborn as a mule."

But she was also down-to-earth and "a whole lot of fun."

Gwen's pep talks were a combination of "common sense, enthusiasm for your hopes and dreams, and an absolute belief that you could do anything you put your mind to." Today, if Mary Kay is facing a challenge, she still hears her mother's voice in her head, spurring her on and encouraging her.

❂❂❂

The best teachers are those who know when to be students. When Mary Kay found herself paralyzed by clinical depression, Gwen would learn a profound lesson—that sometimes life drags you beneath the surface into dark waters; and all you can do is float, look around, search within, and try to understand how you got there . . . until light breaks through and you can start swimming again.

It was the '80s, and Mary Kay had done more than 300 episodes of *Mary Hartman,* as well as films and albums— all without a break. She was burned-out. "I wouldn't slow down, so my body did it for me. I just crashed. It was like the bottom had fallen out. Even though I was trying to get a handle on it with therapy, I couldn't pull myself out of that dark place."

Gwen realized that her daughter's situation wasn't going to be alleviated by the usual "pulling oneself up by the bootstraps" philosophy. Depression renders its victims helpless.

"Mother didn't understand it at first," Mary Kay says. "No one in my family had any experience with something like that."

Knowing she had to rescue her daughter, Gwen flew to Los Angeles from Tulsa, stayed with Mary Kay, and was there for her in every way possible. After a couple of weeks, a moment came that would ultimately transport mother and daughter back into life as they had once known it, although both would return wiser for the experience.

"Toward the end of her visit, I made some kind of defeatist comment, and she gave me a look. Something clicked in her eyes. She never said a word, but I got her message: 'It's time for you to climb out of this. You've got to try harder. I know you can do it. You will do it, and you've got to start now.' And I did. That was the turning point."

Sadly, Gwen couldn't rescue herself from Alzheimer's. Because her own mother had been stricken with the disease, she did know that she was at risk. She started to notice small symptoms a year before retiring from teaching.

"Early on, she began taking the drug Aricept, which did manage to keep her in a holding pattern. Then after Daddy retired, the two of them spent the next 14 years traveling, entertaining friends and family, and basically enjoying their lives. Except for my father, no one else in the family knew about Mother's diagnosis for a long time."

But Alzheimer's is a relentless thief, and its conquest is inevitable. Eventually, as Gwen's symptoms became more obvious, everyone learned the truth.

"But even then," Mary Kay says, "Mother carried on just like she always had. She'd hand her checkbook to the cashier at the grocery store and say, 'I have Alzheimer's. Can you fill out my check? I'll sign it.' Her acceptance of what was happening to her always amazed me. I'm sure she went through sadness and grief in private, but in front of us she just soldiered on, making the best of a situation she had no control over. Just like she always had."

It was one of Gwen's final lessons—that despite everything Alzheimer's steals from a person, it can't touch the spirit.

❂❂❂

So what parts of Gwen live in Mary Kay? Not surprisingly, a strong sense of survival and determination, and a bit of the teacher as well. . . .

"Her empathy and her practice of looking at a situation from another person's point of view has not only helped me in life, but it's helped me develop and understand the characters in my work. And when I'm directing, I can sometimes hear my mother's voice in mine. I also share her temper when something makes me mad or I feel there's an injustice.

"When the women's movement encouraged us to find our voice, I realized how much my mother had provided an early example of that. I don't shrink from conflict if that's what's in front of me. I can express myself, and

I've learned to say no. And yes, I can be a bit bossy and stubborn at times." She laughs and wags her finger in the air. "And then there's the finger wagging. My mother did it when she wanted to make a point, and I often catch myself doing it. I once had a boyfriend who said to me, 'What is that thing? Put that gun away.'"

❀ ❀ ❀

One of the gifts of Gwendolyn Lucille Place's life is that she lives on inside many people—not only her children, but the students she taught, the people who benefited from her wisdom and compassion, and the visitors who stayed longer than they intended to simply because it felt good to be around her. Some people are born to be teachers; and those who are lucky enough to cross their paths linger a while, learn, and are changed forever.

⇛ ⇚

Faye [right] with her mother, Ozie [left]; and her daughter, Felicia

faye wattLeton

Faye Wattleton was the youngest person and the first woman to be named president of Planned Parenthood, the largest voluntary women's reproductive-health-care provider. After 14 years, she resigned in 1992 and is now co-founder and president of the Center for the Advancement of Women, a nonpartisan organization dedicated to research on trends in women's opinions and advocacy for their rights and opportunities.

❋ ❋ ❋

Faye Wattleton's mother was "called by God" to service at the age of 17 . . . her chosen path was that of minister for the Church of God, a Fundamentalist denomination. "Jesus called upon his disciples to leave everything behind and follow him," Faye says. "That's what my mother believed as a literal interpretation of the Bible." Not everyone was thrilled with her calling. Faye's father was essentially disowned by his family because he married a "woman preacher." But the Wattleton family continued to be guided by a woman who saw herself as an instrument of God.

"No smoking, drinking, dancing, or movies," Faye says. And discipline was always couched in warnings about God's wrath. "Sometimes it was hard to know where God stopped and my mother began."

❂ ❂ ❂

Ozie Garrett Bell was born in 1915 in rural Mississippi. Her first name was actually that of a family friend. She was the first daughter after four boys; four more children would follow. Her father owned his own farm, preached every Sunday at different rural churches, ran a country store, and owned two sawmills. It was still a time of deep racial divide in America even though emancipation had formally been declared. Policy is one thing; ordinary life is another . . . and that was still split along the lines of black and white. The nine kids were expected to work in the fields picking cotton, albeit for their own father rather than a slave owner. The sons worked alongside their father in the woods and the sawmills.

Ozie, however, would veer off on another path. At 16, she won a seven-state 4-H competition for an essay she'd written. Her prize was a trip to Washington, D.C., chaperoned by the Madison County 4-H home-extension agent, and the opportunity to read her essay on an NBC radio show called *The National Farm and Home Hour.*

"After that exposure to a world beyond rural Mississippi," Faye says about her mother, "it was really impossible for her to go back to being a farmer's daughter."

Ozie made that quite clear to her parents. She told them that they could beat her every day if they wanted, but she wasn't going to pick any more cotton. She then added that she knew they wouldn't kill her because they were good Christian people who'd been "saved."

Prescient words from a 16-year-old who would soon find her calling.

Her parents sent her north to Columbus, Ohio, to live with a churchgoing family who had a daughter about the same age; that's where they decided she should go to school. It was in Columbus that she attracted the attention of a local pastor who saw something special in the young girl and asked her to give a sermon to the youth of the church, which she did to great acclaim.

"But she also had aspirations to go to New York and become a model," Faye says. "My mother was very beautiful."

Those aspirations were set aside. After Ozie's "call to the ministry," she returned to Mississippi, but nothing could get her into those cotton fields with her siblings. On an extended visit with relatives in St. Louis, Missouri, she met the man who would become her husband.

Ozie and George Wattleton settled in St. Louis; and Faye, who would be their only child, was born after World War II began. War doesn't only happen on battlefields and oceans; it happens inside families. George went off to fight and returned a different man.

"My mother told me that her friends would say, 'Your husband was such a nice man before he went off to war.'"

No one understood posttraumatic stress in those times or even very much about traumatic brain injuries. Faye would never know the man her father had once been before war left him with a "plate" in his head and scars in the deepest folds of his psyche. He did suffer physical wounds, but it was the emotional ones that never healed. While not violent, he was volatile. He worked in factories and as a janitor. Meanwhile, Ozie's ministry was taking off.

Faye looks back on the first seven years of her life as being "the most stable I had known, until I became an adult." During those seven years in St. Louis, the Wattletons owned a two-family house large enough to accommodate several aunts who moved in and other relatives who would occasionally visit. Faye was surrounded by family members who doted on her and a home life that seemed, to a child, like it would never end.

The neighborhood also folded itself around her. Because there was still segregation, it was an all-black enclave in which there was familiarity and closeness and pride.

"The doctor, the lawyer, the laborer all lived side by side. I went to nursery school with our family doctor's son. If I needed cough medicine, I'd run across the street to the doctor's office. A lawyer would stop by to shoot the breeze with my uncle and have a cup of coffee. Mr. MacElroy, who was a housepainter, lived three doors down. . . ."

Because Ozie's "calling" as an evangelist dictated the course of the family, their rooted and dependable life was about to end forever. The Wattletons hit the road for Mom's traveling ministry, although Faye only accompanied her parents during the summers. With each school year, she would move in with a different family, never able to call anyone's house home for very long.

"My parents were on the road all the time, and except for summers when I traveled with them, I was left with church members so I could go to school. As a family tradition, education was highly valued. My mother insisted that I remain in one place during the school year. Her idea was that if I were placed in the home of a church member who was a schoolteacher, I'd be treated well and would get a better education. So from the time we left St. Louis, which was in the summer after the end of my second-grade year, until I was a junior in high school, I didn't attend the same school two years in a row. Once, we did stay in the same town for two years—an all-white town in Nebraska—but I still had to change schools from elementary to junior high.

"I tried to adapt to the changing circumstances, but there were times growing up when I just wished that I could live on the same block for many years, have a bicycle, have a best friend, a pet. I had a parakeet once, but it flew out the window in Nebraska. It was the first seven years of my life when I was surrounded by doting relatives whom I always called upon for comfort in strange and lonely places."

Driven by her dedication to her ministry and Jesus's example to leave everything behind, Ozie didn't seem to have any concept of how hard the nomadic life was on her only child. Of course, she hadn't literally left her family. But there are many ways to leave someone. You can turn away from the longing in a child's eyes, from the flickers of sadness, and leave that child alone with feelings that stay bottled inside.

Still, Faye was a valiant trooper. She graduated from high school at 15 and went to college at 16. At Ohio State University, she got a nursing degree, something her mother did approve of. But a profession that had service to God at its center was what Ozie wanted for her daughter, and that was not to be.

"My mother expected me to be a missionary nurse in a church-run hospital. From the time I was a small child, I always said that I wanted to be a missionary nurse. I don't remember at which point this became my ambition."

Faye taught nursing before returning to graduate school to earn a master's in maternal and infant care and certification as a nurse/midwife. A far different path opened up in her life when she got involved with Planned Parenthood as a board member. She eventually became the executive director of a local chapter and then in 1978 became the national president.

The late '70s were contentious years as far as the issue of reproductive rights for women was concerned, and Faye was on the front lines of the controversy. Ozie's reaction to her daughter's presence in the national spotlight was to pray for her and to ask others to do the same.

"She felt I needed the presence of God in my life to change my views and my work. Neither my father nor I were ever pious enough. Neither of us could ever meet her religious standards. And it was only as an adult, examining my relationship with my mother, that I was able to understand that I never could have met her standards. Being able to examine her expectations and my satisfaction with the person I've come to be was a major milestone for me. I think it's when we become adults that we start to understand some of the scars that we weren't able to feel until later."

Faye remained with the Planned Parenthood Federation of America as president until 1992, at which point sheer exhaustion brought her to the painful realization that she had to quit. She was a single mother with a (then) 16-year-old daughter, and she'd grown tired of the battles and the stress of her position. Her daughter, Felicia, was actually the one she confided in when she knew what she had to do. After the decision was made and Faye's resignation became public, Ozie's comment was, "My prayers have finally been answered."

❊ ❊ ❊

Ozie is now 92. She recently moved back to Mississippi, into a house she built on her original family homestead. With time and age, she's given Faye a few glimpses into her own upbringing. She told both Faye and Felicia a few years ago at a Mother's Day brunch that her own mother used to "whip me for everything I did and everything I didn't do."

Faye says, "She told us that one day she saw her father trying to hug her mother, and her mother wouldn't let him. She asked, 'Mama, why won't you let Daddy hug you?' and her mother whipped her for that. When you're raised like that, it seeps into you. I never remember my mother hugging me. She also never hit me—there was no corporal punishment. But she couldn't show affection—not the way I'm affectionate with my daughter, Felicia. I adored my mother when I was growing up. If she drank from a glass of water and left some water in the glass, I'd want to drink from it because I thought it tasted better than the water in my own glass. I loved watching her preach and seeing people's reaction to her—it was like being the child of a rock star. She was a star in the church."

Now, Faye says, she has the best relationship she's ever had with her mother—in part, she thinks, because her mother is in her 90s. But mostly because Faye has accepted that her mother will always be as she is.

"At her age, perhaps there's a vulnerability that makes her orient herself differently toward other people. Mother is much more conciliatory with me now in ways that she wasn't five or ten years ago. But she is still a force. Who would build a house in rural Mississippi at 92? For some reason, she seems to be at peace now with not being critical of me. If my skirts are too short, she doesn't make commentary. I think she's finally accepted that I'll never play the piano at church services as she had envisioned, I didn't become a missionary in Africa—I didn't live the life she had imagined for me. And I am also okay with knowing that what I have done and much of what I am doing will never be what she wanted for me."

It could be that every mother/daughter relationship is, in the final analysis, a play of shadow and light. Some have more shadows; some are bathed in warmer light. But making peace with one's own history means learning to walk easily past the shadows.

"I in my own mind am okay with the knowledge that this is all it will ever be," Faye says. "And that's another milestone, because we all have a primal desire to have a closeness, an intimacy, with our parents. When you finally put that baggage down and say, 'This is all it's ever going to be, and I can't remake her,' it's very liberating. I'm proud of who I am and what I've done and the contribution I've made, and I'm sorry that she can't fully understand the impact that my life and my career has had on a world much broader than *her* world."

There are those things that, no matter how rocky our paths have been with our mothers, rise to the surface and console us. Faye says, "I don't think I would be who I am or would have accomplished what I've accomplished if not for her."

Some of that—a psychologist might say—has been the result of separating herself from her mother. But Faye can also see the links in the chain, not just the ways in which she needed to break it.

"I learned to speak out from my mother. And I learned to be organized and well prepared. My mother, who never graduated high school, studied the Bible with an almost Talmudic concentration. She could—and to some degree, still can—tell you where any passage or verse in the Bible came from. If I quoted something to her, she'd say, 'Look in Luke 5,' or whatever it happened to be. This came about from decades of diligent study of the Bible for four, five hours a day. And she could do it from both the Old and New Testaments. It was a model for me to always be knowledgeable, and prepared for one's chosen profession. Always seek knowledge."

❄❄❄

There's a biblical verse that kept coming to me the more I listened to Faye's story about her life with her mother, Ozie. It contains the phrase *through a glass darkly* . . .

I had to Google it to learn where to find it in the Bible—Ozie would be quite ashamed of me! It is 1 Corinthians, chapter 13, verse 12:

"For now we see through a glass, darkly; but then
face to face: now I know in part; but then shall I
know even as also I am known."

We want to know our parents, and we want them
to know us. But sometimes we have to be content with
shadows, dark mirrors, and the glimpses that start
to come with time. In those glimpses—those narrow
apertures—we begin to see our mothers in a different
shape, a different mold. Only then can we see how *we* fit
into that mold and, as Faye says, "be okay with it."

→»«←

Lily [right] with her mother,
Lillie Mae; and brother, Richard

LiLy tomLIN

Lily Tomlin has won several Tony and Emmy awards, as well as a Grammy, in her 40-year career. She joined *Rowan & Martin's Laugh-In* in 1969, and her characters have become immortal. She has appeared in many films, including *Nashville* (for which she was nominated for an Oscar) and *Nine to Five*. She has also appeared in several TV series: *Murphy Brown, Will & Grace,* and *The West Wing.* Her one-woman Broadway show was called *The Search for Signs of Intelligent Life in the Universe.*

✿ ✿ ✿

The first thing Lily Tomlin tells me about her mother is that she died a couple of years ago at the age of 91, and that Lily believes it was too soon.

"She really loved life," Lily says. "Even though physically she wasn't well, I just know she wasn't ready to leave."

❂ ❂ ❂

Lillie Mae Ford was born in Kentucky to a farming family, one of the few families prosperous enough to have electricity. It was the early 1900s, when there were still vast stretches of farmland in America. Kids in those wide-open places stared out across fields and dust and rows of crops to daydream about lit-up cities.

Lillie Mae would end up moving to one of those cities—Detroit—when she married Guy Tomlin, also a Southerner, but a boy from poorer beginnings. His mother had died when he was a child, his father was an alcoholic, and he was one of ten children. "A wild boy in the country" is how Lily describes her father's early life.

As newlyweds, Lillie Mae and Guy went off to the big city in the midst of the Great Depression. They had Lily and then her brother, Richard, and both kids seemed to barrel into life like it was one endlessly interesting adventure.

"We were a blue-collar family," Lily says. "We lived in a big old apartment building in Detroit. I know I've gotten some of my characters from there. The people in that building were funny, sad, dear, noble, touching. . . . I loved them. My daddy worked in a factory, drank a lot, as Southern men at that time tended to do. He was very citified, though: he'd wear a hat, a white shirt, and a suit jacket to work every morning—and Florsheim shoes—he loved his Florsheim shoes. He'd change into his work clothes at the factory. My mother was the stabilizing force in the family. She loved being a mother and a homemaker. She was always baking and cooking and trying out new recipes. She'd have her church group over, or her girlfriends for their homemakers' club."

Lily laughs at the memory of her mother's "gumdrop cake"—the candies melting into sugary rivers as the cake baked. Another of her creations was dubbed "pig-lickin' cake." Because it's "so damn good," Lily says. It's a recipe her brother, Richard, still uses.

Despite her attachment to home, her mother decided when Lily was 12 that she wanted to work—not a popular or easily accepted notion in that era. Asserting an independent streak that probably runs deep in every Southern woman's veins, Lillie Mae applied for a job at a local hospital as a nurse's aide.

"My father was not happy about this. It was a very proprietary thing—'My woman is not going to work.'"

But Lillie Mae won out. She wanted her own money to buy herself some nice clothes, as well as things for the house. She quickly shifted positions from nurse's aide to baby-formula maker in the hospital nursery. Lily says, "She loved being with the babies and making formula. She was really happy there."

This other life outside her home would serve her well, as Lillie Mae would find herself widowed at the young age of 54. She never did remarry after Guy died at 56, but she kept busy doing volunteer work and never lost what Lily calls her "sense of fun" and her enthusiasm for being with other people.

❈ ❈ ❈

The obvious question to ask Lily Tomlin is, *Did she get her humor, her comedic talent, from her mother?*

"I wish I had. My mother was much wittier than I'll ever be," she says. "I don't think I really appreciated how witty and clever my mother was until I was about 30 when I taped her talking with some of my relatives."

Lily was already doing *Laugh-In* at that time. Her father had recently died, and she flew her mother and other family members to Los Angeles. Over the course of a few days, she began taping their conversations, and that's when she realized just how funny her mother could be.

Lillie Mae, however, knew early on how clever her daughter was. Lily tells a story about one particular Halloween when she was about 13 that became so entrenched in the lore of the Tomlin family that 50 years later her mother would still bring it up.

"In our apartment building, there were old wringer washers down in the basement and no dryers, so people would hang their clothes on a line to dry. The superintendent and his wife were about five feet tall and 200 pounds. Very short, wide people. My friend Susie and I saw Mr. Yontz's overalls hanging on the line, and we both got the same idea—to each put our legs into one of the pant legs (the pants were so wide, we could still walk) and go to a Halloween party as conjoined twins . . . which is what we did. My mother kept asking, 'Did you steal Mr. Yontz's overalls? You did, didn't you?' And I never admitted it. For the rest of her life, every five years or so she'd say, 'I know it was you who stole Mr. Yontz's overalls that Halloween.' I never did tell her."

Lillie Mae had a secret of her own of a more serious nature, although when Lily tells the story, it still comes out funny. The impression one gets is that in the Tomlin home, pretty much everything ended up being funny.

"When I was about ten," she says, "my grandfather died—my mother's dad—and we went back to Kentucky for his funeral. In those days, in the country, they laid the body out in the home so people from the farms could come pay their respects. It was very common to have a corpse in the living room or the kitchen or some other room, all set up for 'viewing.' I had hurt my foot that summer, so I was kind of laid up, and I was into everything in my grandmother's house. I found an old family Bible, with all this history about our family written in there. On one of the pages there was something about a marriage between my mother and someone I didn't recognize. I took it to her and said, 'Mama, who is this?'

"And my mother got a pen and started scratching out the name. She said something like, 'Oh, that's just some old silly thing my sister wrote; she always thought I'd marry that boy.'

"I think she just didn't want it known that she had been married before. My father was supposed to be the only one ever in her life. When we got back to Detroit, I tried asking my father about it, and he said, 'Go ask your mother.' I never did get the whole story. If she didn't want to tell you something, she didn't. Really, I think it had to do with sex—she wanted everyone to think there'd been no one but my father."

❂❂❂

Detroit is a tough city, and the Tomlins' neighborhood was particularly tough. Both Lily and her brother learned to be streetwise and precocious; Lily admits that their mother had very little "parental control" over them. But fortunately, their adventures were more artistic than illegal.

"We used to haunt thrift shops. My brother, when he was pretty young—12 or 13—bought himself a smoking jacket, and he'd spend half the night after everyone had gone to bed redecorating the living room. He wanted it to look like a New York penthouse—more glamorous. He'd put white sheers on the windows, plug in a fan so they'd billow out, move the furniture around."

And Lillie Mae's reaction?

"She let him do it. But then one night, he sawed the couch into three pieces because he wanted a sectional," Lily says.

And Lillie Mae's reaction to that?

"Well, she was stunned. But the thing is, he did it so well. He put something over the sawed ends so you couldn't see them, and he had the pieces all artfully arranged around the room. My mother would push the pieces back together, put them back against the wall like an ordinary couch, but in the morning he'd have them rearranged again."

The woman whose culinary résumé included gumdrop cake couldn't bring herself to get angry at her son's insistent creativity when it came to home decor. Which says a lot about Lillie Mae's appreciation for talent and whimsical humor.

After Guy's death, Lily bought her mother a house in Kentucky; years later she would move to California for a while and ultimately to Nashville, where she died. Lillie Mae had severe osteoporosis, had broken both her hips over the years, although they had healed, and was losing her hearing. But Lily says her spirit never flagged . . . she still loved life.

❦ ❦ ❦

There is a theory that whoever is meant to be at a loved one's side at the moment of death will be. Likewise, whoever is *not* supposed to be there will find themselves elsewhere—in another state, or even just in another room.

When Lily traveled to Nashville that week, she wasn't thinking it would be the end of her mother's life. She had a three-day break from filming *A Prairie Home Companion* in Minnesota and decided to go for a visit. But at 6 in the morning, with only her daughter by her side (Lily had let the nurse go to bed), Lillie Mae died.

"I'd imagined the moment," Lily says, "and I thought, *I won't let her leave. I'll make her stay alive. I'll tell her not to go.* But I couldn't do anything."

Listening to Lily's memories about her mother, it's

clear that Lillie Mae hasn't gone far. She's there in the laughter and the affection that spill out of every story, every recollection.

"She used to write on notes and letters 'Wake up and smell the garlic. I tried the roses and they didn't work,'" Lily says. "And she loved it that we had the same name, or names that sounded the same. She said it was easier to get appointments at the beauty parlor."

Laughter is enduring—one could say, immortal. It loosens the seams between life and death. We keep our hold on those who laughed with us, who found life to be great fun; and time does nothing to loosen that hold. It's possible to miss people and still feel that they're right there, just a heartbeat away. When you hear Lily talk about her mother, you hear all of that—the missing, the sadness, the love, the laughter, and the fun. It was a rich life that Lillie Mae lived—a life that wasn't extinguished with her death.

⫸⫷

Carnie [left] with her mother, Marilyn

Carnie Wilson

Carnie Wilson is a singer and TV host. She co-founded the group Wilson Phillips with her sister, Wendy, and her childhood friend Chynna Phillips. They recorded two albums and had six top-20 singles. She has also recorded solo albums. From 1995 to 1996, Carnie hosted her own talk show, and she has written several books, including *Gut Feelings* and *I'm Still Hungry*.

❁ ❁ ❁

I magine being the daughter of a musical legend, a man whose songs—whose genius—inspired such prominent artists as the Beatles. Imagine that your father's drug use and emotional problems are equally legendary, that stories circulate all the time about what goes on inside your home. Or outside—there's a story that Paul McCartney once waited out on the sidewalk for an hour for Brian Wilson to wake from a stupor and remember that they had an appointment.

But imagine that inside this home, a very human drama is unfolding—a father who, by his own admission, doesn't know how to be one, and a young wife trying to protect her two daughters from the sadness of a marriage that isn't working.

Welcome to Carnie Wilson's childhood.

"I so appreciate being able to talk about my mother," she tells me. "Everyone always wants to talk about my father, but she's been my rock. And without her, I wouldn't have been able to understand my father and have a relationship with him today."

☙☙☙

Marilyn Sandra Rovell was 14 when she met Brian Wilson of the Beach Boys; he was 18. She went onstage with a cup of hot chocolate; he took a sip, spilled it all over her, and fell in love. Two years later, he proposed to her. At 16, Marilyn became Mrs. Brian Wilson.

"Her parents loved him," Carnie says. "They trusted him. That's why they let her marry him at such a young age. And he adored them. They were this close-knit Jewish family, very warm and grounded and loving. My maternal grandfather was a vacuum-cleaner salesman from East Prussia who escaped the Holocaust on his feet, and my grandmother never learned to drive a car. She was a great cook and argued with her husband in Yiddish. They treated my dad so well, with such affection. He loved the simplicity, the purity, of that family. It was a place where he felt no guilt or shame, where he could be comfortable."

It was everything Brian's family was not. The Wilson home bulged and burned with tyranny, rage, and humiliation. Murray Wilson is credited both with masterminding the Beach Boys' success and abusing his sensitive eldest son so severely that he crippled him with shame and sent him reeling into the refuge of drugs.

When Brian met Marilyn, he not only fell in love with *her,* but with a family that looked like peace to him, something he'd never known.

❁❁❁

Marilyn was 20 when she had Carnie; a year and a half later, she gave birth to Wendy. "She really had three children to raise, though," Carnie says matter-of-factly. "My father just retreated more and more, took so many drugs, sank into his own world . . . for my mother, it was like having a third child. She sacrificed a lot, but she rose to the task. She'd always been mature for her age—wise beyond her years. It was the '60s, so she still wanted to have fun and party, except she also had to deal with the situation at home, which was really a hard one."

Carnie remembers being about five or six when Marilyn explained to her that her father was a genius, but was also a drug addict who was searching for something higher, something spiritual, and he'd gone down the wrong road to find it. He thought drugs would be his release, his freedom from the wounds of his past; instead, they were just another prison.

She told her daughter, "He loves you, but he can't be like other fathers. He can't be the kind of father you want him to be. He doesn't know how."

"I definitely wanted his attention and couldn't get it," Carnie admits. "No one really could. I saw his indulgences at a young age, and as a child, I began my own addictive pattern with food and sugar. But even though it was a really tragic situation at home in so many ways, on the flip side, we had a lot of fun. We were surrounded by creativity, by music; we got to go onstage with the Beach Boys, I had a lot of friends, we'd go skiing in the winter. . . ."

And most important, she was fortified by her mother's emphasis on always trying to look on the bright side, the spiritual side, the kind side—a glass-half-full attitude that Carnie credits with pulling her out of every dark spiral that has threatened to pull her down.

We can drown in many ways—through addictions, sorrows, regrets—but if the person who gave birth to us is the one pulling us above the waterline, survival becomes our inheritance.

"I was really young when my mother started talking to me about karma and how important it is to be kind and positive and live a good life, a loving life. I do that now with my daughter, Lola, and she's only two and a half. I absolutely got that from my mother."

Carnie was five when she began gaining way too much weight and was teased cruelly at school because of it. Marilyn instinctively found a balance between nurturing love and parental guidance.

"She would hold me while I was crying," Carnie remembers, "and tell me that those other kids were teasing me because of their own unhappiness and because someone had taught them to do that. She'd say what's important is who you are on the inside, and she'd tell me, 'You're a beautiful, loving person—don't ever forget that.' But then she'd say, 'It *is* important that you stay healthy, though. It's important that you start taking care of your health now, because if you don't, every year it will get harder.' So every year, I'd go to the doctor and it would be: 'Carnie, you have to get hold of this.'

"My weight has always been my Achilles' heel. My mother addressed it and tried to help, but in a totally loving way. She was trying to keep herself together in a marriage that was crumbling, while still supporting me and trying to help me get healthy."

Marilyn and Brian divorced when Carnie was 11; Carnie, Wendy, and Marilyn moved out of the Bel Air home to start a new life without Brian. But, Carnie says, the breakup was devoid of bitterness or rancor—Marilyn made sure of that.

"My parents were very much in love, and I almost feel like they still are. That's a great thing for a child of divorced parents to hold on to. I feel so sad for anyone from a divorced family where there has been a negative breakup and animosity. It's such a sad thing to think of your parents not liking each other. Thank God I didn't have that. They loved each other, but they couldn't live together because my father was too sick, and it wasn't a healthy environment."

Marilyn was now a young divorcée with two daughters—not an easy role for anyone. So, did she date?

How was that handled?

"She did date," Carnie says. "And it was weird for Wendy and me. But she was very open about it. She would talk to us and say, 'I want to find love again; this is good that I'm dating—it's normal, it's healthy. I deserve to be loved and find someone I can love.' So Wendy and I got on board with that, but then of course we would judge everyone she dated. We'd sneak in and spy on them. I remember spying on her sometimes in the bedroom with a boyfriend."

There is something unique about young mothers with daughters—they tend to grow up together.

"There is a very special bond between me, my mom, and Wendy," Carnie says. "I've always been the big sister protecting my younger sister, but the three of us protected each other. It was a very strong unit and still is."

Marilyn is remarried now, to a man who, Carnie says, "she has a lot of fun with and is very protective of her."

Brian is also remarried, and Carnie credits his wife with helping him reenter a world he'd abandoned—that of music and touring—the world he was born to inhabit.

"My mother is very strong and very proud. Her past has had a ton of pain in it, but she's proud of what she's done with that. She's proud of the fact that she literally saved my father's life. She kept him alive. If it weren't for her, he would be dead. And no matter who each of them is married to, they've had, and still have, this really strong love."

The most significant way in which Marilyn lives in Carnie is in her commitment to finding something positive and hopeful in any situation, no matter how difficult the circumstances are.

"I watch myself when something is going wrong," Carnie says, "looking for the good, telling myself there has to be something hopeful in this situation, even if I can't see it right away. I got that from my mother. She's like this warm little tidal wave. When she walks in a room, people feel her energy and want to know her and be around her. Her warmth is really overwhelming. She's so real—there is nothing phony or bullshit about her."

❂❂❂

Families can break apart for many reasons; divorce often has nothing to do with it. They break because hearts turn away from each other. Marilyn didn't allow that to happen in her family.

"I'm so proud of my dad," Carnie says. "How he reclaimed his life, went back to making music, performing. I've learned a lot from him about survival and will. I know he feels guilty about the years when he wasn't there for us, but I treasure our relationship now."

It's easy for a daughter to get angry at a father who isn't giving her the attention she craves. And it's difficult to accept and embrace the notion that he really is doing the best he can—that whatever circumstances are making him unavailable, he isn't callously or cruelly trying to stay out of reach. Carnie was lucky—she had her mother's guidance when it came to looking past her father's behavior and remembering that he always loved his children even when he couldn't show it.

Long ago, an overweight child wept in her mother's arms after being taunted and teased at school. "Who you are is defined on the inside," her mother told her. "Inside your heart."

That child grew up never forgetting that lesson, never forgetting to look into other people's hearts for who *they* really are. Marilyn Rovell Wilson taught her daughter well; it's a lesson that kept her family bound to one another with love, even through the roughest times.

-»» «-

Mariel [left] with her mother, Puck

mariel Hemingway

Mariel Hemingway is an actress and author. She first appeared in the film *Lipstick* in 1976 with her sister Margaux. She was nominated for an Oscar for her role in Woody Allen's *Manhattan* and went on to star in numerous films, including *Personal Best* and *Star 80*—the story of Dorothy Stratten. She has also guest-starred on many television shows and has written two books.

✤ ✤ ✤

Growing up, Mariel spent many hours "sitting in a snowdrift beneath a fence" outside the family's Idaho home, waiting for someone to notice her absence and come looking for her. No one ever did; and each time, after an hour or two, she would go back inside to the only life she knew—tending to her mother, who had been diagnosed with cancer when Mariel was 11.

"I was basically the only one caring for my mother. My sisters were much older; they weren't always around. And my parents didn't really get along, so my father made a point of not being around too much. He went fishing a lot."

❁ ❁ ❁

Byra Louise Whittlesey, known as Puck, met Jack Hemingway after her first husband, a World War II fighter pilot, was shot out of the sky. She had only been married to him for nine months when he was killed, barely long enough for them to really get to know each other. So in Puck's mind, her deceased husband became mythic—the perfect man, the perfect partner, the love of her life . . . and the tragedy of her life. By her own admission, she was never deeply in love with Jack—she just finally relented and agreed to marry him after he passionately pursued her.

Puck was a wonderful cook, a talent Jack nurtured by sending her to Le Cordon Bleu for further instruction. Julia Child was one of the attendees at their wedding.

Mariel's eldest sister, Joan, was born in 1950; Margaux in 1954. Mariel didn't come along until 1961—the result, her mother bluntly told her, of a night spent drinking.

"My mother was very angry, very bitter," Mariel says. "I think she felt cheated by life—her first husband dying, marrying my father when she wasn't truly in love with him. I've spent a lot of time in my life defending her, because no one else saw her the way I did. There were moments of tenderness and love, and I always believed that those were glimpses into who she really was."

Attempts to do normal things, like have friends over to the house, didn't turn out well. "She'd be really mean to any friends I brought over," Mariel says gently. "She was jealous. She never said it, but I knew she thought, *I'm your friend.* She didn't want to share me with anyone; that's why she'd be so nasty. But all other people saw was her grumpiness. It was so sad, because I always thought, *Why can't anyone else see the sweet side of her?*"

But when did *Mariel* see it?

"I think I've exaggerated the moments," she admits. "I've made them bigger than they actually were, or remembered them as more frequent than they were. I have this really clear memory of resting my head on my mom's chest and her hand is on my cheek. I remember it as if it happened many times, but I know that, truthfully, it probably only happened once. It was just so huge to me, though. The same with the times when she'd thank me or compliment me."

❈ ❈ ❈

Carl Jung said, "Children are educated by what the grown-up is and not by what he says."

Mariel's reality was the prison of her mother's illness, a prison that locked her in, too, as the dutiful daughter, the one expected to wait on her mother, clean up after her, be there for her, entertain her. But she found ways to escape. While Puck never left the house, her young daughter would hike the Idaho trails, sometimes in deep snow, almost always alone, finding refuge and sanctuary in nature. She discovered stillness there, and in that stillness Mariel began to forge a deep understanding of her mother's helplessness.

"I swore I was never going to be like that," Mariel says. "My mother saw herself as an ill person, so she always was. She'd built this persona, and she didn't know how to get out from under it. I know she didn't like being the way she was—that bitter, unkind woman—but she didn't know any other way to live. She was locked in."

As we get older, understanding a parent becomes a dance between experience and insight. We use insight to soften the hard edges of our long-ago experiences. But Mariel seems to have had an uncommon amount of insight even as a young girl, although she would never say that about herself.

"When I was 12, I began praying to God to let my mother live. I really believed my prayers would keep her alive. I said, *God, You must save her.* I knew that the person He'd be saving was the person she was underneath—the good, sweet person who peeked through sometimes. Despite everything, I loved her desperately."

❂❂❂

To be given, at the age of 11, the responsibility of caring for a very sick woman—cleaning up her vomit, her blood; sleeping in the same room with her, watching her constantly—is a punishing burden on a young girl. But children only know the reality that surrounds them, and Mariel accepted hers. She didn't yet realize that other homes were dramatically different—that such things weren't expected of other kids.

It wasn't until she got her first film role at 13, in *Lipstick* with her sister Margaux, that she realized how unusual her life was. The movie came along at a time when Puck's cancer was in remission.

"I went to L.A. for *Lipstick,* and my mother came with me," Mariel says. "Because of all the attention she got from everyone on the set, she was happier than ever, and I was completely caught off guard. Suddenly I didn't have to take care of her, and I wasn't really concerned about her much at all. In fact, I think I was a kid for the first time in a long time. Those couple of months in L.A. were glorious, but when we returned to Idaho, more cancer showed up in her. I felt at some level that it was my fault. I'd dropped the ball; I hadn't been praying for her. That's what kids do when no one communicates with them—they blame themselves for everything."

Her next journey away from home would be without Puck. Mariel went to New York to film *Manhattan* with Woody Allen. Suddenly, people were paying attention to *her*—listening to her, treating her as if what she had to say mattered. At 16, she says, "I finally felt like I could breathe. I think I knew that leaving home was crucial to my survival. Otherwise, I was going to lose myself."

❂❂❂

In many ways, it seems like that trip to New York was pivotal. Even though Mariel would continue the challenge of extricating herself from the patterns she'd grown up with, she began carving out a path for herself that had to do with health, spiritual growth, and happiness.

"Feeling like I deserved to be happy was hard," she concedes. "It took work. I could see my mother's influence in me—the idea that life is basically misery with a few moments of joy tossed in. I had to reverse that and say, 'No, life is meant to be joyful, and sometimes there are unhappy times that come along.' "

Puck never did free herself from her own patterns of anger, unhappiness, and jealousy. When Mariel fell in love with Stephen Crisman, to whom she has been married for two and a half decades, her mother was horribly mean to him. "She hated him," Mariel says, "but it was that same thing of wanting me all to herself, and of not wanting me to find happiness with someone else."

Mariel's first daughter was only eight months old when Puck died.

"The day before my mother died, she said to me, 'I want you to know that you're a really good mother and a really good wife. I see that, and I see how happy you are.' The next day my father called me at 4 in the morning. Before he even spoke, I knew what he had to say: that she'd died. I'm sure she had a feeling the end was near, and that's why she told me what she did."

❂❂❂

We are never, as daughters, that far from our mothers, even after they've died. When Stephen was diagnosed with cancer, Mariel's childhood of caring for Puck rose up in front of her like a shadow that had, for years, been lying in wait.

"I thought, *I can't do this again*. Then I thought, *But I am doing it again*. And in a lot of ways I made it about me. I see that now. Stephen recovered but then got cancer a second time, and that time I dealt with it differently. It wasn't about me going back into a role I'd once played; it was about *him* and how he wanted to treat his disease. He's been cancer free for four years now, and there is something really lovely about having come full circle and having healed on so many different levels."

Mariel has found in herself a deep gratitude for the lessons her mother left behind, even though they are ones scarred by pain. By witnessing a life chained to illness, by understanding the peculiar narcissism that traps a person who is invested in illness, Mariel has committed herself to health on many levels—spiritual and emotional as well as physical.

"I really try to look past the surface to the truth of who someone is and have compassion. That's how everyone wants to be seen. But someone like my mother didn't know how to reveal that part of her. Her wounds went so deep that they came to define her."

By seeing how easily happiness can be kept out of someone's life, Mariel has thought deeply about awareness and joy.

"Once I was watching my two daughters playing when they were young, and they were having so much fun—they were so happy—and I caught myself resenting the fact that joy came so easily to them. I realized that's how my mother felt all the time, and I did not want to go there. That isn't who I ever want to be."

☻☻☻

Sometimes the best we can be is formed by reweaving the cords of our past, tying them out of the way so more light can come through. Mariel is proof of that.

The young girl who sat in a snowdrift waiting for someone to come looking for her was learning something vital about all people, although she didn't realize it at the time. There is a part of everyone, metaphorically speaking, that hides out in a snowdrift, hoping someone will search them out. To live with that awareness, to know we're all alike in that way, is to live with compassion for others.

Puck might not have been able to find such compassion in herself, but despite that, she passed it along as a legacy for her youngest daughter.

-»»-«««-

Candice [left] with her mother, Frances

CANDICE BERGEN

Candice Bergen is a Golden Globe– and Emmy Award–winning actress. She is best known for her starring role as Murphy Brown in the long-running series of the same name, and she currently stars as Shirley Schmidt on *Boston Legal*. Candice has also written articles, a play, and a memoir; and has worked as a photojournalist. Her films include *Carnal Knowledge, Starting Over,* and *Miss Congeniality.*

❂ ❂ ❂

I have a childhood memory of Candice—I might have been about nine or ten. My parents had brought me along to an evening gathering at what I assume (although I don't recall exactly) was the Bergens' home. I'm standing in the backyard, looking toward the house to a stone patio, where Candice—a few years older than I—is sitting with elegant posture talking to several adults. I thought she was the closest thing to a princess that I'd ever seen. She was beautiful, refined, polite, and perfectly dressed. I always felt clumsy and awkward, and nothing I put on seemed to look right. Mothers in that social circle always held Candice up as the exemplary daughter, the girl we should all pattern ourselves after. Not many of us could.

Now, of course, pretty much everyone knows that life inside the Bergen home was a bit, well . . . quirky. Charlie McCarthy, the wooden puppet made famous by Edgar Bergen's talent as a ventriloquist, had his own bedroom and was treated like a member of the family.

"Charlie was referred to as my brother for a long time," Candice says. "Kris, my younger brother—my real brother—wasn't born until I was 15. So I remember mornings at the breakfast table with my parents and Charlie McCarthy, and we'd all be having a conversation."

It's understandable that Candice didn't yet know how odd this was—it was, after all, her version of normal. "I have a perverse pride in it at this point." She laughs. "I certainly know now how weird it was, and I think I'm still processing it."

So did her mother, Frances, ever address this eccentricity in their home?

"She just accepted it. My father was 20 years older than she. And at the age of ten she had lost her father to tuberculosis. So Dad was both father and husband." Frances wasn't about to chide Edgar about treating the wooden Charlie McCarthy as if he were flesh and blood.

❧ ❧ ❧

Frances Westerman was born in Birmingham, Alabama, in 1922. After her father died, she and her mother moved to Los Angeles, and Frances worked on ridding herself of her Southern accent. When she was 19, she attended a recording of a radio show starring Edgar Bergen and, of course, Charlie McCarthy. Edgar, then 39, was smitten with the long-legged beauty. A year later, after a long-distance courtship, they married.

Even though it wasn't unusual in that era for women to become mothers in their early 20s, it's still a young age for taking on the responsibility of parenthood. Did Frances have the patience for it?

"Well . . . I wouldn't say she did," Candice admits. "My nanny, whom I adored, did a lot of the child rearing. My parents traveled frequently, sometimes for a few weeks at a time. But my mother did instill in me great values. She was very strict about curfews and doing chores and things like that. And she was very emphatic about manners. That's pretty significant in this town, where so much is destabilizing and skewed.

"We really began our close relationship after my father died, and then it became closer after Chloe [Candice's daughter with Louis Malle] was born. I think after my father died, I made a choice to just stop it."

"It" being what?

"Torturing my mother," Candice says, although she admits that might be a somewhat extreme characterization. "It was more like engaging her in certain ways. My mother was very talented and would have loved to have had a career. She was deeply frustrated that she didn't. She was a wonderful singer, and she carried around a lot of resentment and frustration about a career that never was. That was often hard to deal with, because her resentment was directed at me—things came way too easily for me. I had a career based on very little talent or ability."

I'm sure most people wouldn't agree with Candice's dismissal of her own talents, but it is true that doors opened easily for her. Doors that her mother wished she could have waltzed through.

"I knew, when my father was gone, I had to step up to the plate. There's just a statute of limitations on holding on to blame. We began to get close then, but when I got married and when Chloe was born, she changed her approach and I changed mine . . . that's when we became real friends. It was such an incredible gift."

Edgar's death was unexpected, but it appears that Frances might have had some kind of premonition.

"The day before he died," Candice says, "she was horribly depressed. She didn't get out of her robe the entire day."

Edgar had left Frances unprepared for a life without him. "She knew nothing about their finances. My father had sheltered her. She had to learn how to manage things, having had no experience. But she was amazing. She just dug in and took on the challenge, and she became an incredibly astute investor. We began calling her the 'stock witch.' She developed an uncanny sense of what to invest in."

When Candice took the role of Murphy Brown and her career was indisputably well established, Frances's pride in her daughter overtook any lingering resentments, although she never spoke about her past frustrations and her unrequited longing for her own career and for stardom.

"I don't think she was conscious of how big her grudge had been or how toxic it had been for her," Candice says. "So, no—we never spoke about that. But with *Murphy Brown,* she became very supportive of my work and very proud of me. And she was a wonderful grandmother. She helped me so much with Chloe, and Chloe loved going over there and spending the night. They'd be up at midnight doing mambo lessons. They were really two peas in a pod."

Frances found a second life with her granddaughter, and a relaxation with respect to the role of parenting that she hadn't had with her own children.

Later, when her health went into decline, she would also find a bond with her daughter that neither of them had experienced before.

"My mother was quite ill for about five years before she died. She had one catastrophic illness after another, and surgeries . . . ultimately she was bedridden. She really went through a lot, and she was such a good sport about it. She had no contact with her friends because she kept a very odd schedule. She'd sleep until the afternoon, so if people called, they couldn't reach her; and when she was awake, everything was a great effort, even talking sometimes. My brother was really heroic during this."

Once in a while, Candice and her brother, Kris, would arrange a dinner at Frances's house for one or two of her friends. They'd have someone fix her hair and makeup, and they would make sure it was an early evening because her stamina was so compromised. But as heartbreaking as Frances's situation was, she and Candice carved out moments that stand now as some of the best in their lives.

"I would go over to her house and get on the bed with her. We'd have dinner together and watch TV; we'd talk and hold hands. It was a great comfort to her, but also to me—and to my brother as well. She had become the mother we'd always wanted—she was there for us in such a wonderful way."

By the time Frances died, her health had disintegrated to the point that Candice says, "It wasn't much of a life." She never went into a facility or a hospital; she was cared for at home. But when it was clear that the end was near, she was taken to a hospital.

"We were all there. At one point, she woke up and saw us all gathered around her bed, and she panicked—there was that moment of fear, but at the end she was really a good sport."

❂❂❂

Candice learned a lot about mothering from the things that were missing from her childhood—physical expressions of love, declarations of love. With Chloe, she says she's told her constantly from the start how much she loves her, and has always been very expressive and affectionate.

But Candice was also able to do that with Frances toward the end. "It was such a relief to finally be able to say 'I love you' and mean it deeply, and to be affectionate with her."

Our mothers are not always able to be the mothers we want them to be, and *need* them to be, when we're growing up. Sometimes they have to learn what it means to be one. But if we're lucky, they do figure it out before they leave this world.

Candice knows how fortunate she is. In the midst of heartbreak—seeing Frances terribly ill and deteriorating—she also watched her mother become more maternal. Part of Candice's journey was understanding that her mother simply hadn't been able to do that when she was younger. There might not have been medicine to cure Frances physically, but the evenings that mother and daughter spent sitting together on the bed, holding hands and talking, healed both of them in a realm much deeper than the physical.

In talking about her mother, and particularly the last years with her, Candice used the word *gift* often. Certainly, the fact that Frances learned to fill up the role of mother was a balm to the empty places Candice had carried inside her for years. But there is another part of that gift—she gave Candice the chance to be a daughter.

It's a delicate dance, this mother/daughter waltz—one that defines so much of our lives and charts who we are as women. Sometimes we master it just in time . . . and that becomes the most important time.

→»«←

Marg Helgenberger

Marg [left] with her mother, Kay

marg HeLGeNBeRGer

Marg Helgenberger's role as K.C. on the series *China Beach* won her an Emmy Award in 1990. She has appeared in numerous films, including *Erin Brockovich, In Good Company,* and *Mr. Brooks.* She currently stars as Catherine Willows in the long-running series *CSI.*

❂ ❂ ❂

M

ost of us know that, at a certain point, there will come moments of role reversal with our mothers—moments when we find ourselves behaving in a maternal way with the one woman who used to have exclusive ownership of that role. It happens with time, with age, and with the cycles of life. The first time it occurs, there is something sweet and startling about it . . . and also a bit sad. Because it usually represents the closing of the circle.

But if that role reversal happens early on, as it did for Marg Helgenberger and her mother, Kay, it can be awkward—a rearrangement of the relationship at a time that feels too soon, too vulnerable.

❂❂❂

Kay married her high school sweetheart, Hugh Helgenberger; and they settled in North Bend, Nebraska, to raise their family. They had three children—Marg is the middle child, born just before the '60s turned America upside down. But North Bend remained a world unto itself. It was as if the '60s were happening far, far away—not in that small, quaint town that didn't even have a movie theater. Kay worked as a nurse, and Hugh was a government meat inspector.

"For a while," Marg says, "he had his own meat plant, but he really didn't have a head for business, so that didn't last long."

The Helgenberger kids had a rural upbringing that would probably be hard to find anywhere these days. After school, they'd take off on their bikes and ride till dusk, until they heard their mother ringing a cowbell to signal it was dinnertime. They lived in a tiny house, but then moved to a slightly bigger one, which the family renovated themselves.

"I remember us all with crowbars, prying off drywall. It was a big project. But it was fun. My house was always the one where my friends wanted to hang out. My parents were very cool, very easygoing. A lot of my friends lived out in the countryside on farms, so after football games they would come back to my house and sometimes spend the night."

But illness intruded cruelly on the family.

When Marg was in college, Kay was diagnosed with breast cancer and underwent a double mastectomy; she was only 46. Right on the heels of that, Hugh was diagnosed with multiple sclerosis (MS).

"There was this series of horrific things that happened to my parents," Marg says. "My mother is a very devout Catholic, and she credits her faith with getting her through that time. I can't dispute that—I think it did. My father was also Catholic, although he questioned more than she did. He was very inquisitive, even questioning the priests about things he read in the Bible."

Hugh's health declined progressively and rapidly over the next few years. MS was devouring him, and Kay needed to work—she had to bring in money. Few families are able to handle the financial burden of catastrophic illness; certainly the Helgenbergers of North Bend, Nebraska, couldn't.

"By the time my father was really ill and in a wheelchair," Marg says, "I was in New York working on the soap opera *Ryan's Hope.* I would come back as often as I could, but it was a rough time for my mother. As it turned out, it was really fortunate that I'd gotten that work—it wasn't what I'd planned for myself. When I was at Northwestern, in a production of *The Taming of the Shrew,* a casting director saw me and wanted me to audition for *Ryan's Hope.* My plan was to stay in Chicago and do theater. But as luck would have it, my salary from the soap opera was able to help my mother out financially."

The subject of money is always a tough one, especially in families. And for a parent to ask one of the children for financial help is awkward for everyone. For Kay and Marg, it's where the role reversal began.

In an essay about her own mother on the anniversary of her death, Anna Quindlen wrote: "What does it mean, to sleep beneath the heart of another person, safe and warm, for almost a year? No scientist can truly say."

And no scientist can say what happens when a mother leans on her daughter's heart, depending on her in ways that are unfamiliar, ways that the daughter doesn't feel ready to accept. On some primitive plane, it upsets the equilibrium.

Marg recalls an incident when she and her mother were in Minneapolis visiting Marg's sister. "We were walking along the sidewalk, and my mother asked me when the check was going to arrive—I'd been sending her money. It was extremely uncomfortable. I felt the tables turn." But Marg was able to temper the discomfort with the only thing that could temper it—understanding. "I knew how panicked she was. My father was in and out of the hospital; she was trying to make ends meet. She was grieving. . . ."

Hugh's health declined to the point where Kay had to make the wrenching decision to put him in a home. But at that time and in that area, there was no suitable place for a man in his 40s with MS. Kay was forced to put him in a care facility for the elderly. It was more than any of them could afford, and the only way the state would pay the cost was if Hugh were single.

"In order to put him in the home, my mother had to divorce him," Marg says. "She went to her priest and discussed it with him. Fortunately, he understood what she had to do and gave her his blessing. But it was so much for her to go through. She's very strong, very tough. And through everything, she's stayed gregarious and fun. 'Peppy' is how I usually describe her."

Kay did end up remarrying about ten years after Hugh's death. Her name is now Kay Snyder, and she and her husband live in Omaha. They are both retired, but Kay does volunteer work and keeps herself busy with friends and family. Her son and his family live closest to her, so grandmotherly duties fill up a lot of her time.

One of the things that also occupies her attention is Marg's career; there is a bit of vicariousness there, but Kay's daughter takes it in with a large dose of humor.

Years ago Marg and Kay participated in a *Barbara Walters* Mother's Day special. Kay was flown into New York and given star treatment.

"I was kind of amazed how at ease she was in that situation, with Barbara Walters interviewing her. And I was also a little surprised by some of the stories she was telling—they didn't exactly match my memories. Barbara brought up a *Letterman* show I'd done where I'd told a story about going on a ride-along with a real criminalist. We responded to a call in which a robbery had taken place. Once inside the house, we discovered a cabinet full of sex toys. I was recalling to Dave some of the gadgets that were there, which we then had to dust for prints. The censors ended up bleeping one of the items I listed. My mother had seen the show, and she knew I hadn't intended to be provocative. But Barbara was kind of looking for complicity in a more scandalous version of the story, and she found it. My mother started describing how she called me up after *Letterman* and said, 'Margi, you know you can't say that on the air.' And that I'd replied, 'I know, but I just did it anyway.' None of which happened. I just sat there and didn't say anything. My mother kind of took charge of the interview—it was very strange.

"Then later that night, we went to see *The Producers* on Broadway. Afterward, we went to Joe Allen for a nightcap. We were sitting at the bar, and someone recognized me—*CSI* had been on for a few years at that point. My mother is very proud of me, and she'll talk to anyone. So she was gushing and everything. Then she turned to me and said, 'So when am I going to get my spot on the show?'

"I went, 'What?'

"She said, 'Well, it's been on for four years.'"

Patiently, Marg explained to her that none of the other actors' parents got parts on the show, nor had they expressed any interest in being on it.

It was one of those other role-reversal moments, when Marg had to be maternal and wait for her mother to handle this disappointing news.

Kay has, however, accompanied her daughter to the Emmys and has been flown out for a few other interviews over the years. Laughing, Marg says, "The problem is, if a year goes by and she hasn't been asked to do something like that, she wonders why. She keeps track of how long it's been."

One honor that Marg got was close to home for Kay. Their hometown of North Bend named a street after Marg. There is now a Helgenberger Avenue. The ceremony brought out the whole town, which is still small, and Kay beamed at the recognition her daughter was getting.

"My son had so much fun," Marg says. "He was smiling the whole time. We even got to tour the house I grew up in—which was incredibly small. It's funny, though; we never felt that way growing up."

Clearly, Marg has learned humor in the life she's lived with her mother. One can almost picture the conversation at Joe Allen and her attempt to explain that no parents are invited to be guest stars on *CSI*. "It was so bizarre," Marg says, laughing at the memory. "Clearly it was something she'd been thinking about for a while. She couldn't understand why she hadn't been asked."

On a more serious note, Marg has also learned resilience from her mother.

"My mother has been through a lot. She's a survivor. And it never dampened her spirit. She's a fun grandmother, always keeping up with the latest hot items that my son and my five nieces might want. She's been cancer free for

27 years now. She's happily married, and she really enjoys her life. I hope I'm that full of life when I'm her age."

Kay also has an independent streak, which has not gone unnoticed, or unadmired, by her daughter. "She can definitely be defiant," Marg says.

Years ago Marg's husband, Alan Rosenberg (they're now seperated), was in the film *The Last Temptation of Christ;* he played the apostle Thomas. The film was extremely controversial and had drawn the ire of the Catholic Church, since it depicted Jesus as having had carnal relations with Mary Magdalene. Petitions and objections to the film's distribution were rampant throughout the country.

In Kay's church, petitions protesting any local screenings of the film had been left on the pews for the Sunday service. Kay arrived at the church early and removed every single petition. Her son-in-law was in that film—he had told her it was a piece of art, and it had been judged and condemned before anyone had even seen it. That's where her loyalty lay. She had made her decision apart from the church's position, and the result was that the congregation on that Sunday morning never got a chance to sign the petitions that had been left for them.

So as a devout Catholic, did *she* see the film?

"She did," Marg says. "And she didn't have a problem with it. It was a work of art, an interpretation of Jesus's life. She took it as that."

☻☻☻

As daughters, we don't really have any control over what lessons or challenges will come to us through our mothers. But we do have a choice as to whether or not we learn those lessons and rise to the challenges. Marg would be the first to say that she wasn't really ready in her 20s to take on a maternal role with her mother. But she did. And she did so with humor and with understanding—two qualities that, whenever we learn them, make life much sweeter.

-»»-«««-

Lorna Luft

Lorna [right] with her mother, Judy

LORNA LUFT

Lorna Luft is a singer, actress, and author. She began performing at a young age on her mother's TV series *The Judy Garland Show*. Lorna has appeared on Broadway and off-Broadway. She wrote an autobiography titled *Me and My Shadows*. In 2007, she released her debut CD, *Lorna Luft: Songs My Mother Taught Me*.

❂ ❂ ❂

Any story about Judy Garland has to begin with Dorothy. We all grew up with *The Wizard of Oz.* But when Dorothy is your mother, the story takes on a different spin. As a child, Lorna Luft had to deal with the expectations of eager friends when they came over for playdates.

"I remember one little boy looking at me after he met my mother and asking, 'What happened?' He thought she'd be in a blue gingham dress with pigtails, singing 'Somewhere Over the Rainbow' and holding a little dog. I didn't get it. I'd seen *The Wizard of Oz,* of course, but when you're a kid, you can't relate to seeing your parent as a kid. Now, I'm so grateful to have that as part of my history."

This seems the appropriate place to mention that Lorna and I briefly went to elementary school together, at The John Thomas Dye School in California. And I vividly remember a parents' day when Judy Garland came to visit. I don't know if I expected the gingham dress, or even the pigtails, but I do remember being disappointed that she was a grown-up.

☺☺☺

Lorna has carved out her own place in the world as a singer and entertainer. She bravely wrote an autobiography, *Me and My Shadows,* chronicling her journey from turmoil to making peace with her past.

She's worked hard to get to where she is now—a woman who can say, "I miss my mother. I have finally made peace with my legacy and have learned to embrace what I was left instead of running away from it."

Losing a mother at the age of 16, as Lorna did, is traumatic for anyone. But when the entire world is muscling in, it can unmoor you, and send you drifting into dangerous waters just to get away from all those eyes. Lorna did drift. And sank deep into rage. But she found her way back. Her footprints on solid ground are her story.

☺☺☺

Lorna grew up far from Oz, far from the mantra of "There's no place like home." There *was* no home when she was growing up. Judy took her three children—Liza Minnelli, Lorna, and Joseph—on the road with her, to be cared for by nannies much of the time while their mother was performing. They lived in hotels and rented houses—show-business gypsies.

"She had to constantly work," Lorna says. "The government garnished her wages—she hardly had any money because everyone stole everything from her. We never had a house, a real home. I realize now, as an adult, how scared she must have been all the time, with children to raise, with the responsibility of being the breadwinner. I definitely don't see her as a tragic figure, but there was a lot of tragedy in her life."

And it began early. Judy's mother, according to Lorna, was "horrific," treating her daughter as a commodity, a paycheck. She was also an alcoholic. Judy's father had died when she was a child, and that absence became a chasm she would, for her lifetime, try to fill with other men—none of them deserving or commendable.

"She had no grounding. She made terrible choices in men—men she thought were going to help her, and they never did. She was incredibly needy. Her needs were like a swamp with no bottom, just endless. She looked at every man in her life as her father, her savior, her everything. And they weren't."

Judy began performing as a toddler, and by her teenage years, the cycle of pills had begun. They were provided by the studios, and Judy's mother allowed it. Pills to keep her weight down, pills to help her sleep.

"She had a chemical dependency that people didn't really understand in those years. It was considered 'medication.'

The pills were prescribed by doctors, so they had to be okay. I think to myself sometimes, *If she were alive today, would she have gotten help?* I believe she would have."

The only help Judy got in those years was from Lorna. But Judy never knew the ways in which her daughter was trying to save her.

"It was my responsibility as a kid to regulate her pills," Lorna says. "I remember sitting in hotel rooms, opening capsules, emptying out the drugs, and filling the capsules with sugar." It was an idea Lorna's father, Sid Luft, had come up with. "I was taught that I had to keep an eye on my mother's medications. I was taught to never, ever call an ambulance, no matter what happened. I was to call my father or someone else—never an ambulance because it would get into the press. I was taught at a young age to lie, to deceive, to manipulate. And that's who I became."

Miraculously, Lorna never blamed her mother, even as a child. "I loved my mother, but I hated that she wasn't like other mothers. I knew she was ill; I knew she had problems. So I didn't blame her—I blamed her disease. What I hated was the alcohol and the pills. A few times she went away somewhere and got clean. They called it 'drying out' in those days. But there was no real help or counseling. When she'd come back from those places, I'd get a glimpse of who she really was. But it didn't last long—she'd go back to drugs and drinking."

There were suicide attempts—razor blades across the veins of her wrist, handfuls of pills—but Judy would always call someone first and tell the person she was about to kill herself. Help would arrive predictably, just in time to save her. So Lorna doesn't believe that her mother was serious about ending her life. In fact, she says unequivocally that Judy wanted to live.

"She always made sure that someone would be on the way. And none of the attempts were made when she was sober, so I really believe it was an aspect of her illness, not a true desire to die."

Still, the toll it took on her children can probably never be measured, although Lorna—in her searching, in her determination to understand, in her desire to break the chain—has tried to scope out the damage.

"We were shuttled into other rooms a lot, but we always knew when something was going on. There was always anxiety. It was like this shadow that loomed over everything. Every morning when I woke up I'd wonder, *How is my mother going to be today?* And every day when I came home . . ."

Children who grow up in this kind of environment learn to be tough. Figuring out how to be tender is a choice that waits for them on the road ahead. Some choose it; some don't. Lorna did learn to be tough, but she always held on tight to her love for her mother, and that became one of her lifelines.

❂ ❂ ❂

Lorna was an ocean away the day her mother died. Judy was in London, in a rented house with her then-husband, Mickey Deans, and sadly no one was monitoring her pills. Her death was ruled an accidental overdose. Lorna, staying at a friend's house in Los Angeles, was given the news by her friend's mother.

"I came into the kitchen at my friend's house, and her mother sat me down and told me. It was already all over the radio and television. I couldn't reach anyone. My father had turned the phone off, and Liza was in New York—she was married to Peter Allen then. I couldn't get hold of her. It was really scary, because I just didn't know what to do."

The next week was, as Lorna describes it, "surreal—an out-of-body experience." As a young girl, albeit a wise one for her age, Lorna was about to learn a profound lesson about her mother's place in the world.

When a legend—an icon—dies, the world grieves. As it should, as is fitting. But if you are the child of that legend, you see hands and arms coming from the four corners of the earth to claim the person they long ago decided was theirs. The grief of strangers crashes in, overwhelms, smothers, dwarfs the grief you feel as simply a child who has lost a parent.

"I found myself comforting other people," Lorna says, still showing a residue of that shell-shocked time. "People who never met my mother were telling me about their loss. Hundreds of thousands of people lined up to pass by her casket, mourn her death, but this was my mother." She hesitates before saying, "You must have had the same experience when your father died."

I did, I tell her. But I wasn't 16. I don't know how I would have processed that experience at such a vulnerable age. I don't know that I could have. Lorna—the girl who'd had to grow up much too fast, who had valiantly tried to save her mother's life by replacing drugs with capsules full of sugar—was getting a crash course in the gritty rules of fame. When Judy died, Lorna was forced to cope with the world's sorrow while trying to carve out some small space for her own. She was expected to be there for legions of fans, offering comfort, but no one thought to comfort her.

"I don't really remember her funeral," Lorna says. "I was there—I know I was there. But when I look at photographs of it, or film, I can't place myself there. I think the psyche just goes numb at times like that."

Lorna went to live with her father—hardly a comforting choice.

"He didn't know how to be a real father," she says bluntly. "He was so consumed with being married to my mother, even way beyond her death. I'm now able to forgive him, but I can't forget."

Lorna was alone inside herself, trying to cope with the loss of her mother, which had so many components to it. Sorrow, yes, but also, she can admit, a small element of relief—no more anxiety, no more jolt of terror every time the phone rang. But then there's this:

"There was also boredom, because suddenly there was no more drama. Which had existed my whole life. Drama is an addiction, too. If there is no more drama, what do you do? You start to create it for yourself."

The road for that was already marked for her—with blinking warning lights and ghosts, but she went down it anyway. She left her father's house at 19 when she got her first role on Broadway, and she never went back. She went instead toward the murky places that had proven fatal for her mother.

"When you're chopping up line after line of coke, you can't really say it's recreational use. I knew I didn't want to end up like my mother. I knew I had to get help."

She did what she believes her mother would have done if she could have. Lorna went to Alcoholics Anonymous and credits that program with helping her turn her life around, although she's very clear about the fact that no program will work unless you want it to. Remaining clean and sober is a choice she makes every day, and she never forgets how it felt to make the opposite choice.

Professionally, Lorna's life onstage also reflects the journey she's taken. "People from the audience come backstage and tell me how proud my mother would be of me. In the past, it would make me incredibly sad. Now I'm able to say, 'I know.' And I'm able to say, 'Thank you.'"

That might not seem huge to the average person, but there is nothing average about being the child of a legend. You spend years running from the huge imprint your parent has left behind, thinking that somewhere out beyond it you might be able to find yourself. Then, if you're diligent and lucky, you realize one day that finding yourself means going back and looking right inside the legacy you ran from. It means having faith that, in that vast territory, you will stumble upon yourself. So the simple "Thank you" that Lorna now says to admiring fans represents a huge victory.

❂ ❂ ❂

The challenges of Lorna's life could easily have pulled her under. Instead, she has broken the chain, not only of addiction but of unhappiness. She has a good marriage; a 24-year-old son, Jesse; and a 17-year-old daughter, Vanessa. Her children never went on the road with her, growing up instead in a stable home environment.

However, breaking the chain in one's family is a tricky thing. It means recognizing, accepting, forgiving, and releasing all that was toxic and negative, while at the same time holding on tight to what was good. Lorna has managed that balancing act.

"My mother was very smart, very funny," Lorna says. "She was self-deprecating and a glass-half-full kind of person. She always believed things would get better. She always believed good things were just around the corner. She really *was* Dorothy."

⟫ ⟪

(Photo) Linda Bloodworth Thomason; (mother) Jerry Davis

Linda [left] with her mother, Claudia

LINDA BLOODWORTH THOMASON

Linda Bloodworth Thomason created and wrote the hit comedy shows *Designing Women, Evening Shade,* and *Emeril.* In 1972, she and Mary Kay Place co-wrote a script for *M*A*S*H,* winning an Emmy. Linda went on to write more scripts for that show as well as many others. In 2004, she published a novel called *Liberating Paris.* She and her husband, Harry Thomason, run Mozark Productions in Studio City, California.

❁ ❁ ❁

Linda Bloodworth Thomason's mother died of AIDS in 1986. She'd been given a blood transfusion during heart surgery, and the blood was tainted. Hers was one of many such stories in the '80s, and all those deaths stand as examples of what should never happen again.

Claudia's life, however, stands as an example of what joy can create.

❧❧❧

Claudia Celestine Felts was born in the tiny Arkansas town of Alicia—with a population of 300. Her future husband, Ralph Bloodworth, one of four brothers, was also born in Arkansas, several towns away. Their paths would not cross until years later, in another state.

The Felts family was one of modest means. Linda has a photograph of her mother "standing by the railroad tracks in her little homemade cotton dress." When Claudia was

13, her mother died, leaving a young girl to wonder about her future with no mother to lean on.

The Bloodworths were quite different. "They were a big, audacious family," Linda says. "My grandfather, Charles Thomas Bloodworth, was an attorney and civil-rights activist in Arkansas. He not only defended blacks, but often brought his clients home and let them spend the night."

The Bloodworth boys all grew up knowing how to use shotguns, and knowing they might at some point have to use their expertise against the Klan, who did not appreciate a Southern lawyer "being cozy with Negroes."

"One day when my grandfather was catching a train, the Klan pulled up with a woman in the car. She proceeded to get out and shoot him in the chest. He survived, but after that decided to move his family to Poplar Bluff, Missouri, where the climate was not as racially charged."

Charles and his four sons started a new law firm in Missouri, and one day Claudia Celestine Felts, who had gone to secretarial school instead of college, walked into the Bloodworth & Bloodworth law firm to apply for a job.

She got the job, and a whole new life.

"She fell in love with my father, and I think he was completely captivated by her," Linda says. "My mother was quite beautiful. She looked like Loretta Young. But she had to conquer this big, tough brood. My grandmother didn't want any of her sons to marry girls who hadn't gone to college. The other boys complied with that. But not my father. My grandmother was completely against my mother coming into the family. Of course, at the end of my grandmother's life, it was my mother who took care of her and ended up being her favorite daughter-in-law."

Fitting into the Bloodworth clan was hardly a small accomplishment, especially for a woman who'd had such a different background.

"It was the largest family law firm in Missouri. These men were Ernest Hemingway types," Linda says. "A little softer-hearted than that, perhaps, but they drank and hunted and fished. They were always debating and arguing about politics and literature and law. They were a huge, unruly mob to handle. But my mom just did it. She was always so easygoing, so calm, and completely appreciative of the simple things, like her garden."

Claudia's first child, Ralph Randall Bloodworth, Jr., was born when she was 27; she had Linda when she was 30. She never worked again outside the home and never wanted to. Claudia Celestine, the girl who'd lost her own mother at 13, wrapped her arms around motherhood and the warm land of home and family.

"Her children and home were everything to her. To have her kids sinking into beautiful, soft, clean white sheets at night; to go get them a cookie; to know that the venetian blinds were scrubbed clean . . . that was it for her. She just made everything beautiful, but she wasn't uptight about it. Her first priority was always for us to have fun. All my friends enjoyed spending the night, partly because she was such a wonderful cook. To look in our refrigerator was a privilege—you'd open the door and just stare in wonderment."

Claudia was always, Linda remembers, "dressed to the nines." But not in a pretentious or formal way.

"She just believed, like most of my friends' mothers, that one should put on high heels, a really swell dress, and earrings to go to the grocery store."

There was one exception, though. Claudia liked to go fishing. She would pull out the fishing gear, rev up their small boat, and motor off with her best friend, a career woman who owned the local hardware store.

Linda readily admits that when she was growing up, she was "a real mama's girl." She remembers trailing her mother around the house when she was a child, waiting for her to sit down so she could climb into her lap. "I adored her jewelry, her perfume, everything about her. We never fought or competed—I know that's strange. It could be that I had a lot of my father's personality—his drive and ambition—so we just blended the same way my parents blended. But it was she who provided the calm, consistently nurturing atmosphere that allowed my brother and me to grow. I guess these days you would say she was very Zen."

Zen was hardly a word that Linda—or anyone else, for that matter—would use to describe her father. While

Claudia and Ralph did have a very solid and romantic relationship—he was all male; she was all girl—it was a case of opposites fitting together well.

"They fought and made up in front of us. Nothing was secret. If he wanted to get back in her good graces after a disagreement, he would slow dance her around the kitchen."

He also brought lively, political conversation to the dinner table, insisting that opinions be expressed and examined. Claudia, on the other hand, focused on setting a lovely table with beautiful linens, flower arrangements, and a well-planned menu.

"And my father drank," Linda says. "He was sort of Atticus Finch, with liquor. He would walk a mile through the snow to return a penny—he was a really good man. He'd practice his final arguments for court in the living room, pacing the floor. On a few occasions, I even rode my bike down to the courthouse to listen to him. But he did drink, and my mother and I would sometimes have to go looking for him. I guess people might think of that as traumatic, but it really wasn't. It was more of a 'girls have to stick together' adventure. He was never mean or difficult—he was actually kind of sweet when we found him. Nevertheless, it made an impression on me that a lot of men in our town did what they wanted and the women often seemed powerless. I used to tell my mom, 'Someday I'm going to come back here and do something for the girls.'"

❂❂❂

Ralph died of cancer in 1982. Linda was about to marry Harry Thomason, and she remembers that the day her father died, her mother's tears were more for her. "Your father wanted so much to dance at your wedding," she told Linda.

It was typical of Claudia to think first of her daughter's loss. But her own was immeasurable, chiseling its damage into her heart. It's common to speak about a broken heart in poetic terms—as an ethereal, purely emotional event. But the truth is, grief can physically break a heart, and often does.

Very soon after Ralph's death, Claudia was diagnosed with a serious heart condition that required surgery. Following the operation, when she should have been getting better, she wasn't. In fact, as time went on, she was getting worse. Linda brought her to California, where a doctor gave the devastating diagnosis: AIDS. She'd gotten it from the blood transfusion she'd had during surgery— the transfusion Linda had agreed to, believing it would be safe.

The year 1986 was a borderline one in terms of the nation's blood supply. There was knowledge in the medical community that it was tainted, and there were high-level meetings in which the blood banks decided it would cost too much to test the blood and clean up the supply. Their secrecy and financial considerations cost many people their lives. All this was revealed in a lawsuit filed by Linda and Harry. But none of that could save Claudia:

she was dying. Linda was given the news the same day *Designing Women* was bought as a series. What should have been a triumphant day was suddenly crisscrossed with shadows.

For the next six months, Claudia lived with the couple while Linda wrote scripts for *Designing Women.* But because Claudia's health was so compromised, they had to repeatedly admit her to the hospital. In those years, terror over contracting the disease from casual contact consumed everyone, so AIDS patients were treated as if they had the plague.

"The nurses and doctors all wore masks and gloves when they were around her," Linda recalls, "as did we. My mother was slipping into dementia, so she couldn't understand why we all looked like that. The nurses would put her medication in a bucket and kick it into the room. There were times when we brought her back into the hospital and we'd hear them say, 'What's she doing here again?' They did not want us there. They wanted her to die."

Linda and Harry finally moved Claudia to the Sherman Oaks Burn Center because there were nurses at that facility who had experience with AIDS patients. When they got there, the nurses hugged Linda and then hugged Claudia. "We all started crying," Linda says.

"My mother was on a floor with about 25 gay men, and I saw so many of them die completely alone. It was horribly sad. It made me think of a war hospital—you'd hear that during the night three more men had died while the television droned on with some insidious game show."

Harry often slept on a cot beside Claudia's bed to monitor her breathing, and both he and Linda became good friends with her doctor. It was a vigil until the day Claudia died . . . with her daughter holding her hand.

"My one regret is that I didn't take her back to Missouri so she could die there. But I kept thinking she'd rally again and we'd have a little more time. After she died, I would call her phone number and let it ring for a long while before hanging up. She didn't have an answering machine or anything modern like that, so I couldn't hear her voice again. But I just wanted to hear the phone ring in that house. There was never a single time when I called my mother that she didn't say, 'Oh, I was just thinking about you.' I had a mother who was always there and who gave me such unconditional love; it provided a template for how I wanted other people—especially men—to treat me. That's a great gift to give a little girl."

In 1989, Linda made good on her promise to "come back and do something for the girls." She called the English architectural firm of Crowther of Syon (the Queen's architect) and asked if they would travel to the Ozarks to build a cultural and educational center in memory of her mother. "I wanted it to be as beautiful as she was," Linda says. Today the Claudia Foundation, complete with Lord Byron's fireplace, serves as a cultural mecca for underprivileged girls and has put more than 160 women through college.

✪✪✪

There is a strange thing that happens when you've watched a parent waste away, when you've seen your mother or father in ways you never wanted to, ways that tear at your heart: after the end comes, those aren't the images that prevail. It's not that you've forgotten them—you never can—it's just that older, sweeter, happier images bloom and spread themselves across the screen of your memory.

This is Linda's enduring image:

When she was in high school, she desperately wanted to be a cheerleader. She practiced the splits in her room constantly; she would do cartwheels down the sidewalk. The day she made the squad, she walked home from school, and as she approached her house, Linda saw her mother standing in the middle of the street—smiling, arms spread wide, welcoming her daughter home.

"Truthfully, I think she was more relieved than proud. She simply could not bear for me to be hurt."

Linda knows she got her drive and her ambition from her father, but she got calmness and balance from her mother. "I never lose my temper," she says. "Well, almost never. And I got that from her. It's a good quality to have in entertainment and politics."

It's a great gift to know that someone is standing in the road waiting for you with arms spread wide, welcoming you home.

※

Anjelica [right] with her mother, Ricki

aNjeLiCa HustoN

Anjelica Huston is an actress, director, and producer who won an Oscar for her performance in *Prizzi's Honor*. She has been nominated twice more and has received five Emmy nominations for her TV work. She won a Golden Globe in 2004. In addition, she has directed several films, and her production company in the Los Angeles area is called Gray Angel Productions.

❧ ❧ ❧

Anjelica Huston walks up the stairs of the large studio space she shares with her husband, sculptor Robert Graham. In her hands is a small plastic bowl containing a carefully folded dish towel and a baby hummingbird she has just rescued from the clutches of one of her cats. The tiny bird appears unhurt; it's looking up at us and peeping. We agree that it was probably just pushed out of the nest by its mother—the abrupt but necessary first flying lesson—and the cat seized the vulnerable little bird. Anjelica places the bowl on a high second-floor balcony where no cats can get to it, and we sit down to talk about her mother, who died when Anjelica was 17.

❦ ❦ ❦

Enrica Soma, who was known as Ricki, was the daughter of an Italian immigrant. She and her four siblings were raised in New York, where her father eventually owned a restaurant after he worked his way up from being a busboy. Tony Soma was a colorful character; he took up yoga in his 30s and had some unusual philosophies and practices.

"I remember when we would go to stay with Grandpa," Anjelica says, "he'd make us all stand on our heads and sing 'Oh, What a Beautiful Mornin'.' It was just part of his routine."

When she was 14, Ricki fell in love with dancing and joined the New York City Ballet. "My mother was very beautiful. She was tall, with dark hair and gray-blue eyes. Very exotic looking—she had a timeless look about her."

At that young age, Ricki would first cross paths with her future husband, John Huston. It was during World War II, and Tony Soma had a speakeasy in New York. A lot of Hollywood people showed up there, and Tony would frequently bring Ricki to the club and introduce her to famous and influential people.

"One night," Anjelica says, "she was introduced to my father. She mentioned to him that each time she went to the ballet, her father made her write a three-page essay about it. 'Well,' he told her, 'I'll take you to the ballet, and you won't have to write anything.' But before he could take her, he was called into the service, so according to him, he ordered a carriage and a corsage so this young girl could go to the ballet in style."

In families of actors, stories are malleable things, and Anjelica is well aware that some embellishments may have occurred in this one. But according to Huston lore, here is how the other half of the story unfolds:

"Years later my mother was performing in the New York City Ballet, and a photographer came to shoot the prima ballerina. He saw my mother and thought she was quite beautiful, photographed her, and her photograph appeared on the cover of *Life* magazine. She was offered a contract to go to Hollywood by Selznick. That's how she ended up here. Tony only told her one thing when she left: 'Don't smoke.'

"Shortly after she arrived in Hollywood, she was at a dinner party at Selznick's, and to her left was John Huston. He leaned over and said, 'I don't believe we've met.' And she said, 'Oh, but we have.' That was the start of their relationship."

John was married at the time to Evelyn Keyes, but they were having some problems—mostly, Anjelica says, over John's two pet monkeys.

"He was very attached to these monkeys, and they'd begun to tear up Evelyn's underwear or something. Then one of them—the female, I think—attacked her. That happened a lot around my father—he had this strange effect on animals. They would become tremendously possessive of him—in this case, to his advantage, because he and Evelyn broke up and he took up with my mother.

She became pregnant with my brother, Tony, before they married. And I was born a year later."

Ricki was a young mother—only 21 when she had Anjelica. But since children's perceptions aren't always based in reality, Anjelica did not see a young woman married to a much older man.

"When I think now of how I considered her—so adult, so authoritative, really quite strict—it amazes me. She was very mature for her age, but still, 21 is so young. She was a lot of fun, though. She was modern, she had a great eye, she loved to dance, and she took me to see Ike and Tina Turner in London when I was about 14.

"But I longed for some kind of solid middle ground. My mother was at times too Bohemian for my taste, not enough of a debutante mother. At other times, too strict. More proper or less proper—I could never decide."

Anjelica isn't sure when things began to get rough for her parents. It's possible that they had never been exactly smooth. John carried on relationships with other women throughout his marriage to Ricki, as he had with his previous wives. He wasn't around a lot, frequently traveling to distant lands. And when he did return to his family in Ireland, Ricki valiantly attempted to become an accomplished horsewoman, to "ride to the hounds." She wanted to impress her husband, knowing how important an equestrian life was to him.

"Riding was a requirement for any woman in my father's life," Anjelica says.

But alas, Ricki was not cut out for this pursuit. Her flexible dancer's body made it difficult for her to stay on a horse. She fell and fell and fell. After one particularly bad experience, when she ended up in a huge pile of pig dung, she ended her efforts to be the horsewoman John wanted her to be.

So she began carving out a life for herself, taking Irish fabrics—especially tweeds—to couture houses in Paris to be sewn into the latest fashions. "I think Ireland was very lonely for her. Ireland was the horsey set, and many of the people around us were older. She had a few friends, but she really didn't fit in."

Sometimes as adults, we find ourselves able to fill in the missing pieces from our childhoods. One of Anjelica's missing pieces has to do with her parents' separation. She now knows it happened when she was 11, but no one at the time explained to either her or Tony what was actually going on.

"We were just told, 'You have to go to school in London now. And your mother will live in London with you, and you'll come back to Ireland for holidays.' We moved into a house with our ex-tutor in a place called Rosary Gardens. He had taught us French when we were children, and he and my mother were friends. His name was Leslie Waddington.

"I hated that flat; I hated the school I was sent to. I was miserable. I began to contract every childhood disease I could. Finally, I managed to fall over in the playground and break some tiny bone at the top of my spine. So I ended up in plaster for months, which I quite liked because then I got some attention."

While Ricki could at times be an attentive, nurturing mother, she was also still a young woman who wanted a life for herself. That resulted in her leaving her children with nannies for significant stretches of time. Anjelica was in tears each day as she was sent off to the school she hated, but no one thought to dry them or even probe the reasons for her unhappiness. She felt utterly out of place in her new school. Even the French she had learned from childhood didn't match up to the more formal French of her classmates. She felt displaced geographically and socially, and home was an uncertain place. Her mother was there, while her father still lived in Ireland, and no one was saying why.

❦❦❦

Both John and Ricki were having affairs, and both ended up adding to the Huston family. John had a son, Danny, and then Ricki became pregnant with Allegra. For a while, the same shroud of secrecy that hung over John and Ricki's separation was employed with regard to these new developments.

"We went to visit my father," Anjelica says, "and he came out and announced, 'Wonderful news! You have a brother.' Then we went home, and my mother was putting on weight and she said, 'Can't you make things easier on me? I'm seven months pregnant.'"

Children who grow up surrounded by secrecy learn early on the architecture of dread. They see life as a poorly constructed home, always apt to topple around them. Anjelica describes it as "a constant feeling of foreboding that was always there as an undercurrent. *What's going to happen next? Who's going to crop up next?*"

And they learn to utilize secrets themselves.

"I didn't talk to anyone about what was going on or how I felt," Anjelica admits. "Not my brother or my friends. I kept everything to myself."

Often the shadows of secrecy that fall across a person's life are, in time, lifted—usually long after childhood, when both parent and child are older. When the roles are less defined, less obtrusive. When conversation flows easier. When old agendas have dropped into the mist.

That's a scenario Anjelica will never know. It was erased from the field of possibility when she was 17.

"My mother was driving with her boyfriend, a man younger than she. They were on their way to Venice from London, and the car collided with a truck. I don't know if she died at the scene, or if she died on her way *to* the hospital or *at* the hospital. I don't know how long she lived."

Anjelica was awakened by Leslie Waddington. They were no longer living at his house. By then, Ricki had her own home in London where Anjelica and Allegra, who was four, were staying with a nanny. Somehow Leslie had gotten the news first, and his way of breaking it to Anjelica was to stir her awake and say, "Wake up. Are you awake? Your mother is dead."

"I'll never forgive him for that," Anjelica says.

She had lost the parent she never expected to lose. "It was the singular biggest shock of my life. It was just impossible. I'd always expected my father to fall dead at any second. He smoked too much, rode too hard, drank too much. He was reckless and fearless, always injuring himself in some adventure. But my mother was never going to die. It never occurred to me that such a thing could happen."

A service was held for Ricki at a Quaker church in London, which Anjelica attended. But then she promptly fled.

"I literally ran away. I didn't want to stay in that house; I didn't want to look in my brother's face or our nurse's face. I wanted to be far, far away."

She went to New York and understudied Marianne Faithful in *Hamlet*. But grief and loss don't stay behind; they follow you across continents and oceans.

"You never get over it," Anjelica says. "Even now. Sometimes it feels like ancient history, but sometimes it feels so immediate."

Death takes more than a life; it steals possibilities, dreams, imaginings of a future. It leaves behind a jumble of history, which takes time and tears to sort out.

"I pour my mother into my work constantly. I think she never had a chance to fulfill her personal strength. She was far more talented than she ever took advantage of. She didn't have the confidence, and she certainly didn't have the support. My father treated her the way he treated most women, and that makes me sad. And a little angry."

Anjelica had a strange but sweet thing happen long after her mother's death. "It was right after Jack Nicholson and I had broken up; and I was very, very sad. Like a dark night of the soul. My doorbell rang—I was living in the canyons at the time—and it was a FedEx man. He had a package for me from my uncle on my mother's side. He had found a framed poem in his attic that my mother had either written or copied when she was nine. It was in her spidery handwriting, and it read: 'The Cedar tree is big and tall, it sways and rocks with the wind. And when the wind goes howling by, I think of the bird with the broken wing who will find the comfort the cedar will bring.' That felt to me like some kind of message. So, I think she's there somewhere."

When we say good-bye, Anjelica goes to check on the baby hummingbird, who will, hopefully, learn to fly without its mother.

As daughters, most of us ultimately do the same. Whether our relationships with our mothers were scarred or smooth, too brief or blessedly long, at some point we travel off on our own wings. But we never stop wanting our mothers to be watching out for us—to feel pride and worry and love. If they're gone, we lean on the mystery, the possibility that they are still there somewhere.

➤➤➤ ◄◄◄

Ruby [foreground] and her mother, Emma

RUBY DEE

Ruby Dee is an actress, poet, playwright, author, and activist. She starred in *A Raisin in the Sun* on both the stage and screen and has appeared in many other films, some politically charged. She won an Emmy Award for the TV movie *Decoration Day* and has been nominated seven other times. With her husband, Ossie Davis, she wrote *With Ossie and Ruby: In This Life Together*. In 2008, she was nominated for an Oscar for *American Gangster*.

✿ ✿ ✿

Until Ruby Dee was 11 years old, she believed that Emma Wallace was her mother. She even thought they looked alike—that she, more than her three siblings, had Emma's strong features. Because Emma's mother was a black Native American, Emma had inherited a sharp profile along with her father's straight black hair, which she braided and coiled into buns on each side of her head.

In Ruby's autobiography, co-written with her husband, Ossie Davis (*With Ossie and Ruby: In This Life Together*, which received a Grammy for best spoken-word recording in 2007), she described the moment when the truth was revealed to her:

> It was a gray day, and I was standing near the piano in the living room when my brother Edward said, "She's not your real mother, you know. Gladys Hightower is your real mother." I didn't believe him. He explained the history . . . as best he could.

The history was this: Gladys Hightower had abandoned her husband, Edward, and their three children. She'd taken off to follow a smooth-talking preacher who promised he could lead her to salvation. Ruby was still a baby when she left, so any memories she had of Gladys were dim and swallowed by time. She had simply accepted that Emma was her mother . . . until that wintry day.

Gladys would eventually reenter Ruby's life—sporadically and never happily. It was a strange duality: two mothers, one who had given birth to her and another who raised her. But Emma was the only one she called "Mother."

❀❀❀

Emma Benson was 13 years older than Edward Wallace. According to Ruby, they liked and needed each other, but there are no signs that it was a great love affair. Emma often used to say to her adopted brood, "I married your father for the sake of you children."

She'd taken pity on the young man who had been abandoned by his starry-eyed wife. Emma even helped pay for Edward's divorce; and when word came back that Gladys was pregnant with another child, also Edward's, Emma decided to adopt that girl, too.

The new family moved from Cleveland, Ohio, to

Harlem. It was 1924—not an easy time to be black in America. Harlem was a nexus for racial empowerment. There were demonstrations; speakers on street corners; and frequent clashes in the streets, many of them resulting in injuries, even deaths. In the South, Jim Crow laws were strictly enforced. If you were black, you sat in the back of the bus, and if you took a train, your place was in the car behind the engine. This was the world Ruby had been born into. It was a world Emma understood and was not about to accept.

At Atlanta University, Emma had studied under W. E. B. DuBois, the well-known black philosopher and historian whom Martin Luther King lauded and frequently mentioned. She then went to Columbia University. She had strong political opinions and refused to accept the racism that was rampant in America. Ruby recalls how Emma took the four children with her to picket on 125th Street outside Blumstein's department store, which had for years refused to hire black people for anything other than janitorial work.

She would also stop on the street wherever impromptu speeches were being given and encourage the children to listen and pay attention. To learn.

Ruby describes Emma as "a no-nonsense mother" and "a resourceful woman."

"She made extra money renting out the spare rooms in our home," Ruby says. "And whenever she got lucky with the horses or numbers, she would rent another apartment in our building and then sublet it to roomers. There weren't many hotels that catered to African Americans then, so people would rent rooms for visiting relatives. Several of Mother's roomers were musicians and artists in town for a short stay. I got to meet a few famous people that way."

Ruby credits Emma with making sure the kids learned music, read poetry, and studied hard. Emma, who had at one time been a schoolteacher, was determined to lift her children above what white America expected and encouraged them to become.

Children want attention and approval from their parents, and they will choose the avenues that lead to that fulfillment. Ruby learned to play the piano and the violin; she wrote poetry and studied hard enough to be able to show off her talents and report cards to company. "It was a great source of pride for both of us," she recalls. She went to Sunday school, later to church; she folded her clothes, made her bed, and kept her corner of the apartment neat and orderly.

But children are also keenly aware of what's missing. In her autobiography, Ruby wrote:

> There was a distance between Emma and us children. She wasn't the kind of mother into whose arms we rushed; she didn't grab and tickle us or laugh out loud and play with us. She rarely hugged, kissed, or showed her affection, but I believe she loved us.

The times Emma was able to show affection stand out prominently in Ruby's memory.

Ruby was a frail child, having contracted rickets early on. She had convulsions as a result and was frequently sick. She recalls one night when she was so ill that she couldn't come to the dinner table. She heard Emma ask, "Where's Ruby?" And then Emma came for her and found her huddled on a chair; she picked the girl up in her arms and carried her to bed.

Ruby remembers, also, when she was about four years old, dropping and breaking her new china doll. Her sobs moved Emma to lift her up and hold her tightly until her tears dried. "In that moment," Ruby says, "I sensed her love for me."

Those moments are touching to hear about, but they were rare. Still, Emma was the mother Ruby looked up to and adored.

She was a mother who was determined to inspire and encourage her children, and Ruby didn't disappoint her. She went to Hunter College High School and later got into Hunter College. She credits Emma with spurring her on, as well as educating her about speaking up in the face of injustice. Many years later, Ruby Dee and Ossie Davis would become strong voices in the battle for civil rights and racial equality.

❂❂❂

Throughout much of Ruby's life, Gladys Hightower would show up for brief visits, as well as send candy and gifts occasionally. As a teenager, Ruby admits that she felt contempt for the woman who had abandoned her family. But it became obvious that Gladys had serious problems—many of her letters were about God, spaceships, and Communist devils.

As Ruby got older, her contempt was replaced by tolerance and even sympathy. On one visit in 1955 when Ruby and Ossie were already married with two children, Nora and Guy, Gladys begged to take Nora for a walk, and Ruby allowed it. On that walk, she asked the child to please call her Grandma Gladys. Nora did, and when she got home, she told Ruby about the request. "Just don't let Grandma Wallace hear you say that," she warned her daughter.

To her credit, Ruby can now say that she spots certain physical traits in herself—movements, speaking patterns—that were inherited from Gladys. Even though Emma was the woman who mothered Ruby and her siblings, Gladys is part of them. Her blood flows through their veins. Beyond the difficulties of a scattershot history, Ruby has found the sweetness that comes with acceptance.

Gladys died in 1965, shortly after phoning Ruby to say she would be leaving soon on a spaceship. She died in the ladies' room of a Detroit movie theater. Ruby and her sister LaVerne went to Detroit and arranged her funeral.

It closed one chapter in Ruby's life, but nothing closes out one's memories. Sometimes when Ruby hears herself speak, she is reminded of Gladys's voice. Sometimes when she looks at her children or her grandchildren, she sees a movement, a shift of the shoulders. . . .

❦❦❦

Emma died in 1970 while she was visiting Ruby and Ossie. As often happens when a loved one is about to die, Ruby felt a strange and unfamiliar anxiety that day. She had an appointment with an acting coach, which she kept, although she felt removed from the whole experience. And then she kept a lunch date, during which she tried to call Emma, but she was told that her mother was asleep. She didn't want to wake her.

Later that day, Nora found Emma on the bathroom floor where she'd fallen. Ossie carried her to the couch, and they got a doctor who lived across the street to come over, but it was too late. Emma was gone. She was 87 years old.

He broke the news to his wife that night at the theater (she was performing off-Broadway in *Boesman and Lena*), and Ruby suddenly understood why she'd felt so out of sorts all day. The only woman she'd ever called Mother was gone, but Emma had left her imprint on Ruby's soul and on her life. Her wish for the children she'd adopted was that they rise up and be the best they could be, and Ruby fulfilled that dream.

❂ ❂ ❂

Ruby Dee had to accept the complexity of two mothers: one who didn't know how to be one, and another who wanted to take on the task but who found encouragement more comfortable than affection.

Emma Wallace and Gladys Hightower both live in Ruby—in different ways, deeply and permanently. Her acceptance of the two women who shaped her in so many ways is a testament to the choices she has made in her life—she could have chosen bitterness, but didn't.

"The older you get," Ruby says, "the more you realize how deep the mother/daughter relationship is."

It's not clear when she says it which mother she's talking about, but then, it doesn't matter. She has embraced both of them.

→» «←

Julianna [left] with her mother, Francesca

Julianna Margulies

Julianna Margulies is an Emmy Award–winning actress best known for her role as nurse Carol Hathaway on the series *ER*. Since leaving the show, she has worked regularly on the stage and the screen. She starred in the TNT miniseries *The Mists of Avalon* and appeared in *Searching for Debra Winger*, as well as on several episodes of *The Sopranos*.

✿ ✿ ✿

Julianna Margulies is the daughter of a creative, free-spirited mother—a dancer—who thought it made much more sense to spend money on a trip to India than on mundane items like a washer and dryer. As the youngest of three girls, Julianna has inherited some stories that she was part of but can't actually remember because she was so young when they occurred. Like this one:

The three girls were living with their mother in Paris (Julianna's parents separated when she was an infant), and her mother was dating a man who had a pet monkey. One evening, wanting some time alone with each other, her mother and the boyfriend put the animal in the girls' bedroom . . . *with* the girls.

Waking up suddenly to find a monkey on her head, Julianna started screaming. Her sisters then began screaming, and the monkey joined in. Their mother opened the door and asked, "What is all the ruckus in here?"

They shrieked at her that there was a monkey in their room, and she said, "Oh, for goodness' sake, kids, it's just a *little* monkey."

❁❁❁

Francesca Gardner enrolled in the School of American Ballet (SAB) when she was seven years old. She lived in Brooklyn, and every day she would take the train into Manhattan by herself to study dance.

"Ballet saved her life," Julianna says. "That's what she always said. She hated school, her home was not a happy place, and she felt that ballet allowed her to escape a Brooklyn life that would have trapped her. Manhattan to her was mecca; it was magic. She stayed at SAB until she was 18, and then she joined the American Ballet Theatre company."

❁❁❁

Francesca's mother was a pianist, and her father owned a beauty salon. The marriage was fraught with tension, in part because Francesca's father had a number of mistresses. Her parents eventually divorced.

While dancing in *My Fair Lady,* Francesca, then in her 20s, met Paul Margulies on a blind date. He had studied to be a lawyer, but what he really wanted to do was write poetry. It was the beginning of the '60s, and revolution was everywhere—on the streets, in homes, and in the air. The desire to find a different way of life separated generations and left confused parents watching helplessly as children took off for distant lands with too little money and too many dreams. To his mother's horror, Paul quit law, became a vegetarian, and started studying biodynamic farming. Once he and Francesca were married, they took off for Israel.

"My father was searching for his path in life," Julianna says. "And I really think that both of them were trying to get as far away from their parents as possible."

Francesca gave birth to her first daughter, Alexandra, in Israel—an experience she describes as "horrible."

"She was 24, she had no family there, and the hospital wouldn't give her anything to manage her pain. They just told her to scream."

So, Israel didn't work out for them. Francesca, Paul, and Alexandra returned to New York and made their home on the Upper West Side. Paul got a job in advertising as a copywriter, and they had their second daughter, Rachel.

"My mother loved it," Julianna says. "She was back in her element, they had their friends around, there was family nearby. And then . . ."

A decision was made to move to the suburbs— a decision that Francesca claims ruined everything. It was a trend at the time, moving from the big city to the outlying areas, so the family relocated to Spring Valley, New York, which was where Julianna was born in 1966.

"Suddenly my mother was picking my father up from the train; he was commuting 45 minutes every day—he hated the commute. She said it was the unraveling of their life because all of a sudden she was stuck in a house. Instead of taking her daughters to Central Park and being with all the other chic mommies, she was a suburban housewife. She was a ballerina, and she felt caged in. I get it now—I didn't when I was younger."

Francesca and Paul separated when Julianna was one, and he moved to Paris, where he wrote perfume jingles for an advertising firm. After a year, the rest of the family followed, which for Francesca was a godsend.

"It got her out of the suburbs; the kids got to be near their dad. . . . It was heaven for my mother—it was freedom. She had men right, left, and center." Although with Francesca's dating life, Julianna says, "thus unfolds a tricky relationship between mothers and daughters."

Less tricky for Julianna than her sisters. Alexandra, as the oldest, bore the brunt of everything. She longed desperately for a more grounded, ordinary life; she would grow up to get married at 22 and have two kids by the time she was 28. "She wanted a different life. She just wanted stability. We didn't have that. We had a lot of other things, and we were always loved, but we didn't have stability."

As a two-year-old in Paris, French became Julianna's first language. But the '60s restlessness still burned in both Paul and Francesca. After two years, he got a job in

London, and she decided to study at Emerson College in Sussex. She wanted to learn eurythmy, an art form of speech and music through movement that was developed by Rudolf Steiner. It would become her life's passion, something she still teaches.

"So my first language was French," Julianna says, "and my first accent was British. I refused to speak French when we moved to Sussex because I didn't want to be different."

But she would soon have to learn how to lose her British accent. When Julianna started first grade, the family moved again—back to the States, back to New York, and for Francesca and the girls, back to the suburbs. Paul lived in Manhattan and worked at another advertising firm. He would become famous for the Alka-Seltzer ad ("Plop, plop, fizz, fizz . . ."). Francesca continued studying eurythmy in New York.

"It was a golden time for me," Julianna explains. "I felt very secure, even though my mother had a gazillion boyfriends. Alexandra used to answer the phone when they called and say, 'My mother doesn't love you anymore,' and hang up. As a child, you either get attached to these guys or you hate them, but as the youngest, I wanted everyone to be happy, so I didn't cause too much trouble. I loved my school in Spring Valley; we spent weekends with my father in Manhattan—I felt like I had the best of both worlds.

"My mother's most serious boyfriend in those years was my gym teacher, whom I adored. And we rented out the basement to a friend of his, who taught me how to play guitar. We didn't have a lot of money, and we didn't have a television, so we'd put on plays . . . we always had people there; the house was always full of music. I remember that time really fondly. Then when I was about ten, my mother knocked over the cart. She said, 'I'm sick of the suburbs.' She did that again. And this time she decided she wanted to move to Germany."

Francesca rented out the Spring Valley house and went to Nuremberg, Germany, without the girls, leaving them with Paul while she got settled. But just before they were supposed to join her, she phoned him hysterically crying and said that she hated Germany—she couldn't stay there. "Send the kids to England," she told him.

"She'd gotten a job working at a school for mentally handicapped children," Julianna says. "So that's where we went. That was the story of our life: everything was always disorganized. Alexandra refused to go and stayed in New York with our father. Rachel and I got on a late-night flight—she was 14 and I was 11—and we ended up back in England for the next two years living with the mentally challenged children.

"My mother could never figure out the driving situation in England. She was always on the wrong side of the road; our cars were always these beat-up things that kept ending up in ditches. She was always late. I was thrilled when I got to seventh grade because then I could walk to school—I didn't have to rely on her to take me. I am now the most punctual person in the world—I mean, to the minute—because my mother was constantly late."

❂❂❂

Julianna and Francesca have talked about the past. "We've had great talks about it, actually, and we've moved on. The truth is, I always felt loved; and, yes, it was unconventional, but it made me who I am. And it's not like I didn't always feel like I had a roof over my head—I just wanted more stability. So I created it wherever I went. My best friend is someone I met in England when I was three years old. It's been two years since I've seen her, but the two of us could sit down and talk until the sun came up the next morning. We'll be bonded together for life.

"I have a family of friends all over the world. And I have a different sense of respect for that kind of unity than I would have if I'd just had a mom and a dad who never moved around. I think it's why I'm an actress—I love putting on other people's shoes."

❂❂❂

Julianna is now a new mother. She had a son, Kieran, in January of 2008. Recently both her mother and her mother-in-law came to stay for a few days and help take care of the baby.

"It was so beautiful to see them with him—two people who love him as much as I do. I understand now what my mother has always said: that no one cares what your temperature is the way your mother does."

Francesca may have been an unconventional mother— one who couldn't be bothered with the required uniforms when the girls went to school in England. "She used to send me to school in my riding blazer instead of the mandatory blue blazer—I was mortified. She just thought those details were silly." But . . .

"She was also a mother who, when I was a teenager and I crashed her car—I'd looked down to change the radio—never got angry. The first thing she said was, 'Are you okay?' The material things didn't matter to her; she just wanted to make sure I wasn't hurt."

Some daughters have to wait a while for their mothers to settle down and fully inhabit their maternal roles. Here's a story from when Julianna was in her 30s, one that *doesn't* involve a pet monkey:

"I was doing a play in Poughkeepsie, New York, and I was staying at a dorm, so I brought my laundry to my mother's house. My mother had finally gotten a washer and dryer. I put my laundry in and lay down to take a nap. When I woke up, my mother, who sings so beautifully, was singing and ironing my shirts with spray starch. I looked at her and said, 'Mom, I don't know if I woke up in the wrong house.'

"She lifted up the starch bottle and said, 'I got this at Kmart—it's fantastic!'

"I went, 'Who are you?'

"And she told me, 'You know what, honey? I'm ready to be a mother now. I was too young; I wasn't ready. I loved you all, but I didn't want to iron shirts—I wanted to go out and see the world.' That to me was the beginning of our adult relationship."

Julianna has found that she listens to her mother now in ways that she didn't before and is better able to appreciate the wisdom Francesca has to offer—some of it in small gems like, "When in doubt, don't."

"When I was in my 20s, I didn't take what she said seriously because I was annoyed with her—she wasn't solid enough for me to have respect for her. It wasn't until my mid-30s when I gained incredible respect for her because I accepted who she was. And I realized that the only person I could call at 6 in the morning after I'd been up all night worrying about something was my mom. The truth is, if you want to have a relationship with your mother, you have to accept who she was in the past and move forward."

✵ ✵ ✵

There is a quote of Rudolf Steiner's (the man whose teachings Francesca has spent decades studying) that could apply to the journey of her life. He said, "A truly artistic nature welcomes everything that could possibly serve to widen and enrich the whole field of art." For many artists, life and art are intertwined. As the daughter of just such an artist, Julianna has come to appreciate the richness of an unconventional childhood—one full of unpredictable moves, a pet monkey in the bedroom, a few cars run into ditches . . . but always the certainty of love.

-»» «««-

Diahann [left] with her mother, Mable

DIAHANN CARROLL

Diahann Carroll is an actress and singer. She has appeared on Broadway, and both in films and on television. In 1968, she starred in the TV show *Julia*—she was the first African-American actress to star in her own series where she wasn't playing a domestic worker. Diahann won a Golden Globe for her role.

❂ ❂ ❂

When Diahann Carroll talks about having needed, at a certain point, to separate herself a bit from her mother, she isn't referring to her adolescence—that pouty time when girls typically flounce away from their mothers and shut the bedroom door behind them. Or maybe the front door. She's talking about a time deep into both of their lives when it was simply necessary to have a little breathing room between them. Diahann and Mable were always extraordinarily close; the friendship that many of us find later on with our mothers was one that she had from the start.

"We had our tiffs and disagreements sometimes," she says. "But if there was a bottom line that had to be dealt with, I always went to her, and she always came to me."

❧ ❧ ❧

Mable Faulk was born in North Carolina to a strong, courageous woman who carried on after her husband was killed in a farming accident. Proud and unafraid, she took her produce into town to sell at the market even though she was the only black woman there.

"My grandmother learned to be a survivor during a terribly rough time in this country. She was extremely strong and very determined, and I'm not sure my mother really paid homage to her until she was much older. But they, too, had a very close relationship."

Mable's mother raised hogs and grew tobacco as well as cotton; she made ends meet, but there was no money left for education. The church in their small town set up a collection so that Mable could go to school. "But," Diahann emphasizes, "it certainly wasn't a good school. The difficult thing for me was to grasp that my mother was dealing with very little information, since she had virtually no education." Still, she stresses that her mother carried herself with great dignity and pride.

By her early 20s, Mable was married and living in New York—in Harlem, to be exact, although she didn't like the way that sounded.

"She insisted on calling it Morningside Heights," Diahann says, laughing at the memory. "No one else called it that but my mother."

Diahann, who was born in 1935, remembers Harlem at that time as being very family friendly and even elegant in a quiet, understated way.

"The brownstones were lovely. It was a family-oriented place then. Children spent holiday weekends at each other's houses. We had picnics. It was almost formal in some ways. My mother wore gloves to church. And there was great respect for the minister, who was Adam Clayton Powell, Jr. He had married my parents, and my mother was very proud of that. I was baptized in the church when I was a baby, in my long satin dress."

Diahann's father, John Johnson, who also had little education, had a gift for numbers; and while he worked as a motorman in the New York subway system, he and Mable stayed up nights going over tests so he could work in insurance. That never materialized, but John was able to put his financial talents to work by buying some properties in Harlem and converting them into rooming houses.

Fourteen years after Diahann was born, her sister arrived. "My mother was a little surprised," Diahann says, acknowledging that 14 years was a long time between babies.

When World War II began and many women took jobs to help in the war effort, Mable insisted on working occasionally, as long as she could be home when Diahann came back from school.

"This did not go over well with my father," Diahann says. "He would always manage to talk her out of it."

At an age when many girls don't want to hang out with their mothers, Diahann and Mable spent a great deal of time together. They would go shopping at Macy's and stop for hot dogs at the stand just outside the store.

"We weren't supposed to. We were supposed to be home getting dinner ready, but it was our little adventure. We were always really, really close friends." She pauses before adding, "I don't know why it is, but I think many of us who had especially close relationships with our mothers have had trouble getting close to men. I certainly have in my life, and I've observed it in others."

That may also have been true for Mable. Even though she did have a loving marriage, she enthusiastically embraced her daughter's career and did eventually get divorced. She never remarried, which probably further cemented the bond she had with her eldest daughter.

Diahann has been married several times, to both white and black men. She recalls the time when her mother just had to ask: "One year it's a white man; the next year it's a black man. Do you ever get confused? Do you ever wake up in the morning and look at him and wonder . . ."

Diahann, perfectly at ease with the question, responded, "Mother, I don't marry a color. The man beside me is my husband, not a color. He's a person with a character, a personality, and that's all I see."

Mable pondered this for a moment and said, "Oh, I never thought of it like that. Now I see."

It's the way friends talk to each other. It's the way I think every daughter dreams of talking to her mother—maybe not when she's younger, but eventually. Diahann is among the lucky ones—she always had that smooth path between her mother and her, a comfort level that permitted such intimate exchanges.

❃❃❃

Professionally, as a performer, Diahann has spent a lot of time on the road. "My whole life, I've always been the traveler. And my mother would go with me, or I would send for her. She was very involved in my career. Everyone who worked with me adored her. They treated her like she was the queen of the Nile or something. And she just loved it."

But as Mable's health declined due to heart problems, going on the road with her daughter became impossible. She stayed behind at Diahann's house, but efforts to provide her with round-the-clock care kept hitting some snags.

"She would fire everyone," Diahann says. "She would say, 'You're not needed,' and turn them out. And then she'd tell me, 'Diahann, you mustn't do this. You're trying to make me old before my time.' I realized I had to move her out of my house and into an apartment so I could do what her doctors were telling me to do. I had to explain to her that I couldn't keep being called back from tour dates and performances because my mother had fired all her nurses."

That was the moment when Diahann realized that, for all their closeness, she and her mother needed a little more space between them, in part so that Diahann could make some of the hard decisions that children often have to make for aging parents.

It's a delicate dance that many of us are faced with—how to ensure that our parents are cared for and out of danger without making them feel humiliated. We find ourselves having to enforce certain guidelines, we become parental with our parents, yet we don't want them to feel diminished.

Mable fought it for a while, even in her apartment, which Diahann had decorated beautifully so it looked like a warm, welcoming home. She resisted the idea of having night nurses, but eventually she relented.

For the last year of her life, Mable was essentially bedridden and no longer argued about having round-the-clock care.

"My mother had a rough time of it," Diahann says. "She didn't want to let go. She was a fighter. I think she knew I did everything I could for her. She always felt better when I was around. Even toward the end, I could see in her face when I came in—*Oh, my daughter's here. Things will be fine now.* I had to tell her, 'I can't make you well. I can be here with you, and I know we have this bond, but I have to do as your doctors have told me to do.'"

There was one sweet sideline to that period of Mable's life. Diahann's father, who had by then divorced his second wife, came to see Mable several times, and according to Diahann, they "realized they had never truly gotten divorced from each other."

Diahann was at the Music Center making a speech the day her mother died. She had seen her the day before; Mable's apartment was just down the street from Diahann's house.

"When I got offstage, I saw the faces of the people who were with me, and I knew my mother was gone."

John Johnson passed away peacefully in his sleep just weeks before Diahann and I spoke. Fortunately, she had been able, after many years of distance, to reclaim a relationship with her father.

❂ ❂ ❂

Diahann sees a lot of Mable in herself. Strength and determination, certainly, but there's another trait that she knows has her mother's stamp on it.

"When I'm confronted by a problem or situation that has to be dealt with, I'm a little bit too stubborn about it. I think sometimes, *I don't have to be quite that stubborn.* So, I'm trying to be more open-minded. I hear myself sounding just like my mother sometimes. Some of these things just penetrate your brain, and you don't realize it for a while. I try to tell myself, *Just be open and listen—there might be another way that's more conducive to everyone.* I'm still stubborn, but I'm trying."

Mable was also very involved in her wardrobe, as Diahann has been throughout her career. And to her amusement, she sees some of that in her five-year-old granddaughter. (Diahann has a daughter, Suzanne, and two grandchildren.) It doesn't take a scientist to see that even things like a love of fashion can be passed along in strands of DNA.

❄ ❄ ❄

Henry Ward Beecher wrote: "The mother's heart is a child's schoolroom." Diahann Carroll learned about strength and dignity from her mother; most important, she learned about friendship and loyalty. Mable Faulk may not have had a formal education during her life, but her heart provided the best possible schoolroom for her daughter.

⟫ ⟪

Marianne Williamson

Marianne [right] with her mother, Sophie

MARIANNE WILLIAMSON

Marianne Williamson is an internationally acclaimed lecturer and best-selling author, most recently of *The Age of Miracles*. She has done extensive charitable work, including founding Project Angel Food in Los Angeles. She is also the founder of The Peace Alliance, a nonprofit organization dedicated to fostering a culture of peace.

❂ ❂ ❂

M

arianne Williamson's mother passed away barely a month before we spoke. It's in the raw days after a parent dies that we find ourselves living fully in his or her presence, often more so than we ever did before. Like many of us, Marianne was emotionally estranged from her mother at various times. Now she regrets that she didn't spend more time with her during the last years of her life.

❂❂❂

Sophie Ann Kaplan was born and raised in Houston, Texas. She attended college at the University of California, Berkeley, and then returned to Houston. At 21, she married Sam Williamson, a major in the Army during World War II who later became an immigration attorney. Together, they traveled the world extensively. Sophie's first child, Marianne's older brother, Peter, was born when she was just 22. Two daughters followed, Marianne being the youngest.

It was a fairly traditional '50s home. Sophie didn't have an outside job or career; her work was raising three children and taking care of the household—work that Marianne now sees as getting "short shrift" by those who devalue what is involved in being a stay-at-home mother. Marianne says, "The fact that she took care of the house, my father, raised three children the way she did—I'm finally at a point in my life where I see that that's not only the most *important* work there is; I also see that it's the *hardest* work there is."

Through the clearer lens of years, Marianne has come to reevaluate many things about her mother that she didn't appreciate, recognize, or even acknowledge in the past.

"I remember when I was a little girl how much I adored my mother, and I remember the break that occurred when I was a teenager. I look back on it now with a sense of sadness. So much time was wasted, and so much wisdom that she could have and would have imparted to me had I been willing and able to listen to her. The trust between us broke—at least on my end. The cord of that trust was so severed that I simply couldn't hear my mother.

"But there were pockets of my life when I could and I would. There were times throughout the years—after I left home and would come back to visit—when she would come into my room late at night before she went to bed. She'd sit at the end of my bed, and she would just talk to me. I adored her at those times. I'd think to myself, *If only she would be this way all the time, we'd have such a great relationship.* I think now that it was both of us who needed to drop the masks we wore. They kept us from having authentic, soul-to-soul conversations most of the time. But then late at night, when she would sit on my bed like that, our masks would drop and she would seem wise to me.

"In my family, I was the girl who felt like she didn't have a voice, who felt like she had to escape, to separate herself from her family. But I never didn't love my mother. . . . I always craved those times when we would find each other."

Marianne and Sophie's relationship began to mend when Marianne became pregnant.

"When I first told my mother I was pregnant, her initial reaction was how terrible it was that I wasn't married. And she'd call nearly every day with anxiety and stress over that fact. After a few days of this, I said to her, 'You know, I really want you to be part of this experience. I want you to be my mother in this. I want you to be a grandmother to my child. However, you need to know that your being positive about this is extremely important to me. I can't have negativity around me now. So, this is the way it's going to be. I am having this baby, and I am not getting married. And if you can be positive about it, I really want that. If you can't be, I can't have it, Mom.'

"And she switched on a dime. From that day forward, every word she said to me was loving and encouraging. She called me every day during my pregnancy, and I was so grateful for those calls. She was there in the hospital room after I came back from delivering my baby. She was there in the early years of my daughter's life, helping me, and it was priceless to me. It really was my daughter's birth that brought my mother and me back together again."

Whenever Sophie visited, Marianne was struck by how kind and gracious she was to her friends. Occasionally, when people would congratulate her on Marianne's success, she would respond, "Well, she was very difficult to raise," but there was a twinkle in her eye when she said it. Marianne didn't doubt that her mother was proud of the woman she had grown into, both personally and professionally. "Both of my parents were very supportive of my career."

❁ ❁ ❁

When I interviewed her, Marianne was living in Houston, but one of the things that haunts her is the feeling that she should have moved there years ago. "I went back when my mother got ill, but she was much closer to the end at that point than any of us knew. I regret deeply that I didn't go back sooner. I live with the same sense of sorrow and regret that many people do that I wasn't there more for my mother at the end of her life."

Marianne's older sister died of cancer not too long before her father died. She watched her mother go through the overwhelming grief of losing both a child and a husband. There is an exquisite helplessness in witnessing your own parent's grief; you see that parent, maybe for the first time, as utterly human, separate from the confines of their defined role. Nothing you can do will lessen the pain of loss, but there is a great richness—for both parent and child—in finally seeing your mother or father through clearer eyes.

It's hard work to step back and look at both your childhood and your parents' lives in the context of time and social realities. It often feels like a cross between therapy and archaeology. But it's work that Marianne hasn't shied away from.

"My mother was born in 1921, and I'm a child of the '60s. I have a social reference now, which has allowed me to understand what my mother was afraid of, what she felt threatened by. But my parents didn't need to worry as much as they did about me because they had instilled certain values in me when I was very young, and I was never going to deviate that much from them no matter how much external drama I was manifesting.

"I had an interesting background. I grew up in a very liberal household, but at the same time a very Southern one. My mother had been raised in Houston, but my father was from the Midwest, with a mix of political liberalism and social conservatism. So I was raised to wage the revolution, but with my white gloves on. And when I was little, those white gloves were literal. What I see now is that my parents' generation spoke in different symbols than mine did. We just spoke a different language."

She can now empathize with how Sophie saw her youngest daughter's efforts to be an individual, separate from familial influences, and how distressed she was.

"There came a point in my life when my mother looked at me as someone who had taken away her little girl. 'I don't know who you are, but I want my little girl back. I want Marianne back.' I used to resent her for that. But now I look back and I see that she was exactly right. It's like an impostor had taken over. I'd lost my authenticity. I think in many ways my mother saw me more clearly than I saw myself."

❀ ❀ ❀

Sophie's health was in decline for several years. Shortly before her death, Marianne moved back to Houston. She remembers being in an airport when she got a call from her brother saying that their mother had taken a turn for the worse. She found herself sobbing uncontrollably in the harsh public space of an airport.

"People were so kind. They were bringing me water and comforting me. I had completely fallen apart when I got that call."

Sophie lingered for two more weeks. Marianne recalls that, at some point during her illness, her mother told her that she had come to believe she would see her husband again—an idea she had previously shunned. She didn't elaborate on how her belief about this had changed; she only made clear that it had.

"I do feel that she is with my father and my sister and her parents, and that gives me great comfort. And I believe they'll be waiting for me someday."

As far as how Sophie lives on in Marianne's heart and soul and daily life, she says, "My mother was very strong. She had strength, dignity, and stature . . . and she had honor. Both my parents taught me ethics, my mother every bit as much as my father. I realize how absolutely ignorant I was to underestimate her or her life choices when I was younger. It's clichéd, but it's true—you simply don't know until you know. Now that I truly see what a good and honorable woman she was—and can appreciate more fully what that really means—I can honestly say that there are many ways in which I want to be more like her. My mother left a tremendous legacy. I feel that I'm called upon now to be a stronger and better person."

❂ ❂ ❂

We form inside our mother's womb, far from her arms but right beneath her heart. It's that beating heart—so close to our own—that some of us eventually run from, believing we can leave it behind. Believing we have to leave it behind in order to discover who we are. But the emptiness swallows us, and we return to the heart that never stopped waiting for us.

The night before Sophie died, Marianne lay down beside her and asked forgiveness for ways she felt she'd let her down. In the aftermath of her mother's passing, while there are years that still wound and always will, the years of closeness and trust are the ones that bring sustenance.

"I think what death does," Marianne says, "is distill everything to its essence. You realize, in the end, that there really is just love."

→»»«««-

Whoopi [left] with her mother, Emma [center]; daughter, Alexandra; and granddaughter, Amarah

WHOOPI GOLDBERG

Whoopi Goldberg is an actress, comedienne, and TV host. She has won an Emmy, a Grammy, an Oscar, a Tony, and two Golden Globes. She has appeared in many films—dramas and comedies—including *The Color Purple* and *Ghost*. She had her own talk show for a year and is now one of the hosts of *The View*.

✿ ✿ ✿

Whoopi Goldberg has no idea how old her mother is. "I've asked and asked—so has my brother—but she won't tell us. My mother is like a clam. She's told us nothing about herself. She always felt that there was no need for her to tell us about her life when we had lives of our own to start looking at. That was really her philosophy: 'I don't need to tell you about me, because it is what it is. But what are you going to do for *you?*'"

What about peeking at her driver's license?

"She never got one. She doesn't drive."

❀ ❀ ❀

Emma raised her two children—Whoopi and her brother, Clyde, who is six years older—in Manhattan. She was a single parent who never discussed the whys and hows of that.

"It was what it was," Whoopi says. "In those days, it wasn't a conversation you had with the kids. My mother is quite eccentric, which shouldn't come as a surprise. She's the reason I am the way I am. The belief system I have comes from her. But there are aspects of her that are still a mystery. If I ask her about herself, she'll tell me I don't need to know that. 'What would it accomplish?' she'll say. After a while, you just give up because you know you won't get anywhere by asking."

When Whoopi was growing up, Emma was a Head Start teacher and a nurse, and while pursuing higher education, she rode her bike to college.

"My mother really is the finest woman I know. She's curious about the world; she's very funny. She had a cousin with whom she had a tight relationship, and when they'd get together, they'd do voices—they'd talk in these dialects to each other, which is where I get it from. I can still hear those routines in my head."

It was pretty clear early on that Whoopi would go into the performing arts, and she wasn't going to get any pressure from her mother to do something different. There were no admonitions about getting a law degree to fall back on, or learning a business. Emma never tried to discourage Whoopi from her creative pursuits. Her only warning was, "You have to be really good at what you do. You can't be half-assed."

Whoopi says, "I was very lucky in the way I was raised. My mother would say, 'If you think you're doing something wrong, you probably are. I don't need to be in your face saying you're doing something wrong; you know better, and I expect you to act accordingly.' She gave us lots of respect and demanded respect in return."

Whoopi's brother, Clyde, now coaches kids' baseball teams, but she says that he, too, is very funny. "He's really dry, and he's the hippest person I know. When he's walking down the street, if you listened carefully, you'd hear his theme music. That's how cool he is."

☻☻☻

One of the most important things Emma imparted to her children was empathy for other people. In their family life it was often emphasized, and it's something that Whoopi knows has guided her in her own life. She tells the following story as an example:

"When I was a kid, we went on a school outing, and my mother also went along. I was not a popular kid—there were sometimes a lot of tears for me because I didn't understand why I wasn't like everyone else. I wasn't hip; I wasn't cool. But every now and then the hip, cool people would look at me and befriend me; and on the day of the school trip, they did, and I was hanging with them. I had a friend who was like me, who also wasn't cool, named Robert; and under normal circumstances, Robert and I would have hung out and laughed and kept each other company on the outing. This time, because I was in with the cool kids, I didn't do that."

Not only did Whoopi not hang out with her friend, she participated when the cool, hip kids started teasing Robert.

"At the end of the outing, I said to my mom, 'Wasn't that great? I had so much fun—I loved it.'

"And she went, 'Oh, good.' I could tell something was up by the way she was responding. Then she said, 'Do you think Robert had a good time today?'

"I asked her what she meant, and she said again, 'Do you think Robert had a good time today?' I knew instantly what she was saying, and I really didn't have an answer for her.

"She told me, 'You know what that's like, you've felt that, and you forgot. You just forgot. Try not to forget again.' And I try not to. That's how she taught me ethics. She's an incredibly ethical woman; and that, I think, I get from her."

❦❦❦

The one time Whoopi took a large detour around the ethics lesson and lied to her mother is an experience etched indelibly in her memory.

"I loved the ballet, and in New York when I was a kid, you could go see the ballet for not a lot of money. In winter at Christmastime they put on *The Nutcracker Suite*, and I was offered the opportunity to go. My mother said, 'Okay, but you have to clean your room before you go.'

"She was going out, and I said I would. But as soon as she left, the Bad Whoopi showed up and said, *Oh, she won't be home for hours—just go.* And the Good Whoopi was going, *Don't do it; don't do it. Just clean your room—it's really simple . . . you've got the time.* But the Good Whoopi lost, and the Bad Whoopi got the keys and the little bit of cash I'd stashed so I could get on the bus. I left and I enjoyed my time at *The Nutcracker Suite.*

"When I got home, I felt for my keys and I felt again . . . and I had no keys. I'd gotten into the building, but I couldn't get into the apartment. And I started coming up with the most ridiculous ways to take care of it, like kids do. *Can I climb out the window in the hallway and walk along the ledge?* But I just had to wait until my mom came home—I had to stand in the hallway and wait. Then I saw her coming down the street, and it was like she could see me, even though I knew she couldn't. But I thought I saw her see me, which was not possible.

"So the elevator comes up, and she says hi. I say hi. And as I'm speaking to her, I'm trying to get around her, and she has suddenly grown 16 feet wide. I cannot get around her; I cannot get over her—I have to now follow her in, which was not what I wanted to do because I'd thought that if I could somehow get in there first, I could use my supersonic speed and clean my room before she got to the back of the apartment.

"She asks me how *The Nutcracker* was, and I tell her it was beautiful; it was lovely. Then she asks if I cleaned my room, and I swear to you, I meant to say no. I wanted to do the noble thing. But I didn't—I just lied. That was the first and last time my mother wailed on me. Because it wasn't only that I'd lied, it was that it was a stupid lie. It was that I didn't think enough of her to at least be amusing."

Emma believed lies were a waste of time, that it was just easier to tell the truth. Because in one way or another, if you lie "you get your butt kicked." Whoopi only needed to learn that lesson once.

❂❂❂

Emma currently lives in California. After working her whole life, she now sits in her garden, reads, and enjoys what Whoopi calls "her leisure time."

"She doesn't like it when I say that I wouldn't be the person I am if not for her," Whoopi says. "It's not that she doesn't welcome the compliment; she just doesn't adhere to this. She feels that for me to give her that credit is to take away from myself. She feels that I got to where I got and I am the person I am, not because she taught me, but because that's who I am. And I say to her, 'But you have to be shown and taught; otherwise how can you know?'

"For me, she taught me right from wrong and then expected me to remember it. With all the people I've met in my life and all that I've been exposed to, I wouldn't trade my mother for a million bucks. Not for a day or a minute."

❂❂❂

It's apparent when Whoopi talks about her mother that she also got humility from her. Which is not something Whoopi would acknowledge about herself . . . people with great humility never do. But it takes more than a little wisdom and bravery to accept that there is a cloak of mystery over wide swaths of your mother's life.

The older we get, the more we long to know who our mothers were before we came along. We want to be able to imagine them in the context of a specific era, a time in history that influenced them socially and ideologically. It helps us fill in the missing pieces; it allows us to understand how the woman who gave birth to us became that woman.

There is a faint note of sadness when Whoopi talks about all that she doesn't know—the geography of Emma's life that has remained in shadow, and perhaps always will. But you have to listen hard to detect the sadness. The gratitude for all that she learned from her mother—ethics, empathy, respect, kindness—chimes the loudest.

-»» ««-

Cokie [left] with her mother, Lindy

Cokie Roberts

Cokie Roberts is a senior news analyst for National Public Radio. She is also a political commentator for ABC news. She writes a weekly syndicated newspaper column with her husband, Steven Roberts, and is the author of several best-selling books, the most recent being *Ladies of Liberty: The Women Who Shaped Our Nation.*

❂ ❂ ❂

"he mind-boggling thing to me," Cokie Roberts says, "is that my mother went to Washington, D.C., as a 24-year-old with two babies. And it was pre–World War II Washington, which was still filled with the protocol of wives having to call on other wives on a daily basis—cabinet officers' wives, Supreme Court wives, Senate wives, House wives. It was a very structured, formal life. And here was this 24-year-old woman with two young children. . . ."

❂❂❂

Lindy Boggs was born Marie Corinne Morrison Claiborne in Pointe Coupee Parish, Louisiana. She went to Tulane University in New Orleans, where she met Hale Boggs when they both worked on the school paper. They married in 1938 when she was 21. Hale left a law career to run for a congressional seat, which he won, and in 1940 the course of their life changed from private to public.

The two children who came with them to Washington were Barbara and Tommy. Cokie was born in 1943, three years after the family began their life in Washington and two years after the entry of the U.S. into World War II. Hale lost one reelection campaign and joined the Navy as a liaison between it and Congress. But it was still a life steeped in politics for the Boggs family.

"One of the things that was very clear in my growing-up time," Cokie says, "was that the political wives—people like my mother and Lady Bird Johnson—ran everything. They ran their husbands' campaigns, they ran their offices, and they ran the social-service agencies in Washington because there really wasn't any city government at that time."

Cokie has never known life without politics, but she says, "Fortunately, I liked that. We all did. My siblings and I all became involved in politics in one way or another. And my mother was very involved. She was my father's campaign manager; she helped run the voter-registration drives."

It doesn't seem like there could have been time or room for the Norman Rockwell–type scenario of Mom standing at the stove fixing dinner when the kids came home from school. . . .

"You know, it's so funny because, of course, in reality I know intellectually that she wasn't there all the time, but in my emotional reality she was always there. We had a housekeeper, a wonderful woman who fixed dinner most nights. But my mother was always the mother who came to get us when we were at school putting out the school newspaper or rehearsing for a school play. She'd be the judge for the debate team—she did all those things. So there was never a sense of her being absent. And we as children were involved in my father's political campaigns. My father determined early on that if we were going to have family time, we had to be involved in politics."

Through years and generations, politics took hold of the family. Cokie's sister, Barbara, worked as a letter writer for President John F. Kennedy; ran for a Senate seat; and then became mayor of Princeton, New Jersey. Tommy also ran for public office and is now a lobbyist in Washington. While Cokie is the only one who hasn't run for office, she's still closely aligned with politics, having established herself as a respected political journalist and author.

❂❂❂

But the one to whom the full weight of politics ultimately fell was Lindy.

On October 16, 1972, Hale Boggs, who was then House majority leader, boarded a private twin-engine plane in Alaska with Representative Nick Begich of Alaska; Russell Brown, Begich's aide; and the pilot, Don Jonz. They were flying from Anchorage to Juneau to attend a fund-raiser for Begich. In the fog and chill of that day, the plane disappeared. Despite an intensive 39-day search by the

Coast Guard, the Navy, and the Air Force, no trace of the plane or its passengers was ever found.

Lindy was at home watching television. She dozed off and was awakened by the phone. It was the Speaker of the House, telling her that Hale's plane had vanished. A few seconds later, the news came on TV. As a nightmare was beginning to unfold, there was at least that sliver of a gift—that she hadn't heard about it from a network broadcaster.

The family flew to Alaska and stayed for several days while the military searched in vain.

"It wasn't naïve to think they might be found," Cokie says. "There are so many stories about planes going down in Alaska and people surviving—being found days, even weeks, later. We believed that that's what would happen. But of course the more time that went by, the less likely that seemed."

After 39 days, the most massive search in the U.S. military's history was called off. The family held a memorial service in New Orleans—an attempt to come to terms with what seemed to be the end of a life. But it's primal to want death to be tangible. After 9/11, the victims' families cried out for something—anything—to stand as proof that their loved ones' lives had ended that day, in that place. A shoe, a wallet, a body part. Anything. Hale Boggs and his fellow passengers simply vanished into the white icy air over Alaska, leaving more questions than answers. If there is no boundary line between life and death, we dream on into the wilderness. And we dream about life.

"We still have the house I grew up in," Cokie tells me. "And years later, I didn't want to change the wallpaper in the kitchen. I thought, *What if he comes back? What if he's had amnesia all this time?*"

Life has to go on even after tragedy and death. So does politics. Hale was reelected to Congress despite being "presumed dead." And then in 1973, Lindy won a special election, taking over her husband's congressional seat. She would remain in office until 1991.

To this day, she doesn't speak of her husband as having died. She speaks of him as having disappeared. Yet there was a moment when she said she knew in her heart that he was gone. She was on a flight to Iran, and she hadn't yet written a speech that she was to give there. Suddenly, the speech came to her completely intact, as if it had already been composed. To her, it was a sign that Hale was looking out for her from a place beyond this world.

It's probable that no one, not even her children, witnessed the full weight of Lindy's grief. Pride and stoicism are important to her even in the face of tragedy.

"My mother is a strong Southern woman," Cokie says. "And she believes that showing emotion is a sign of weakness. So if a person is visibly upset after someone dies, my mother will say, 'They're not being good.' And if someone is holding it together, she'll say, 'They're being very good.' She has a very deep faith—we were raised Catholic—and that's helped sustain her."

☙☙☙

Lindy's faith would be tested again years later, and it would mark her voluntary exit from Congress.

It was 1990, and Barbara, by then married and mayor of Princeton, was diagnosed with terminal cancer. Lindy knew that she couldn't go out campaigning and doing the job of a congresswoman when the place she needed to be was at her daughter's side. She made the choice she needed to make and prepared to lose another family member.

Years earlier Barbara had been diagnosed with cancer in her eye. Just hours after going through surgery to remove her eye, she arrived at a political event in a red dress with a matching red eye patch. Her color-coordinated eye patches became legendary, as did her optimism and her refusal to feel sorry for herself. She never thought that cancer would strike her again, yet it did. And it came back with a vengeance.

"My mother got to Princeton the day before Barbara died. I was already there. The night she died, Barbara's husband came in to us and said, 'I think she's gone.' We went into the room, and my mother had a moment of revealing how difficult this was. . . ."

Her eldest daughter was actually not the first child Lindy had lost. "She lost a full-term baby three years before I was born," Cokie says. "He lived only a few days. But of course losing Barbara was so much harder."

By any objective standard, Lindy Boggs has had a fair amount of tragedy in her life. But don't ever tell *her* that. At 92, she would still bristle at the suggestion that she was victimized at all by fate or by life's unpredictable turns.

"She would be furious if someone spoke about her as a victim. She'd say, 'How could you say such a thing when I've been so blessed?' And of course that's true—she *has* been blessed. She's had good friends, good family, good health, the creature comforts that go along with being moderately well-off, and lots of public acclaim."

When Lindy was 81, she was appointed as ambassador to the Vatican by Bill Clinton. At an age when most people want to put their feet up, she was embarking on a new career.

She lives in Washington, D.C., now, close to both Cokie and Tommy, as well as to 9 of her 18 great-grandchildren. She still has a house in New Orleans, right on Bourbon Street, which she returned to after Hurricane Katrina. The house had only minor damage, but Cokie points out that it's too hard now for her mother to make her home in the city.

It seems that strong mothers breed strong daughters. There is, of course, no scientific evidence for this, no DNA test. But if one were looking for some powerful anecdotal evidence, one need look no further than Lindy Boggs and her daughters. Lindy took the raw clay of tragedy and molded it into tensile strength; it's a gift of sculpturing that not everyone can master. Barbara also remained victorious over cancer in the most important way—it never vanquished her spirit. And Cokie has established herself as not only a best-selling author, but a prominent figure in the field of journalism, which is frequently brutal and even cutthroat—not a job for sissies.

"My mother was the great guilt eraser, rather than the guilt inculcator," Cokie says.

Cokie was covering Congress as a reporter while Lindy was still in office. With two young children at home, Cokie felt the guilt familiar to most mothers who work outside the home.

"It would be getting late, and I wanted to get home to my kids. I'd say to my mother, 'Can't you get your co-workers to go home?'

"And she'd say, 'Your kids are fine. Your kids are doing great. Don't worry about them.'

"That was very different from most of my colleagues. And it was a great lesson to me with my own daughter. My mother's support for me and for what I was doing was terribly important to me. I would feel very proud of my daughter and my daughter-in-law under any circumstances because they're terrific women, but what I learned from my mother is that it's important to voice it—to tell them what a great job they're doing, and what terrific kids they have, and how hard I know it is. My daughter does a two-hour live radio show and then comes home to three little boys. That's hard work, and I really appreciate it and admire it.

"Also, my mother taught all of us entirely by example. She hardly ever said anything about how we should behave; she just made it clear by how she behaved what her expectations were for us."

In probably the most poignant tribute a daughter could give to her mother, Cokie says, "When I am being my very best self, I am being my mother's daughter."

❀ ❀ ❀

There is a bridge in Louisiana that spans the Mississippi River in St. Charles Parish. It's called the Hale Boggs Memorial Bridge. It's a fitting tribute, this wide and sturdy bridge between a rushing river and an endless sky. It's a tribute not only to him but to the family who lost him.

Grief is a bridge we build over losses that could drown us if we let them. It takes years to build that bridge. It takes tears, the ache of memories, the fire of faith, and a fierce amount of strength. Lindy Boggs taught her children how to do that—not through instruction, but through example. Throughout her life, she just kept building.

⇒≫ ≪⇐

Anne [left] and her mother, Katherine

(Anne:) Becket Ghioto; (mother:) Anne Rice

aNNe RICe

Anne Rice is one of the most widely read authors in modern history. She is best known for *The Vampire Chronicles*. The first book in the series, *Interview with the Vampire,* was published in 1976. She has written many other books and has also published adult fiction under the pen names Ann Rampling and A. N. Roquelaure. Most recently, she has written two novels chronicling the life of Jesus, as well as a memoir.

❂ ❂ ❂

a

nne Rice was given the birth name Howard Allen O'Brien by her mother. It was a combination of her father's name and her mother's maiden name.

"She thought it was a wonderful idea," Anne says of her mother. "She thought it was exciting. She thought it was a mark of distinction. She wanted her daughters to have wonderful lives, and she thought that it would be a great asset. But in the first grade [in Catholic school], I told the Sister at the desk when we went into the classroom that my name was Anne. My mother just looked down and said, 'Well, if she wants to be Anne, call her Anne.' She showed the same kind of freedom and liberal attitude when I changed my name. From that day forward, everyone called me Anne."

❂❂❂

Katherine Allen was born in New Orleans, one of eight children, but only three would live to adulthood.

She traveled when she was younger, had many boyfriends, and went to formal balls in New Orleans and events at the Yacht Club.

"She was something of a Southern belle," Anne says. "And she was very moral. She always said you should never let a man kiss you until he puts a marriage ring on your finger. She would talk about her adult life before marriage as being a lot of fun. She did work at secretarial jobs but only until she got married."

Writers are lucky if they have good stories within the boundaries of their own lives. The story of how Katherine met her future husband, Howard O'Brien, is a good one even if, as Anne admits, it might not be true. No other version exists to argue with it, so we'll go with the one that was handed down:

Katherine and Howard grew up in the same church parish; their families were acquainted. But they first met in a school play at the church.

"She was playing the Virgin Mary, and he was playing St. Peter. At one point, he bowed to her and his hair was full of powder—they always made St. Peter look like an old man. The powder made a big cloud in the air. She laughed out of one side of her mouth, and he vowed at that moment to make her laugh out of the other side. He said he fell in love with her right then."

They married when Katherine was in her 20s, and they stayed in New Orleans. In 1939, she had her first daughter, Alice. In 1941, two months before the U.S. became involved in World War II, Anne was born. The O'Brien home, like many in America, was about to change dramatically.

The day Pearl Harbor was bombed, Howard enlisted, and Anne wouldn't get to know her father until she was four years old. In fact, her first memory of him is the day he came home from the war. He was in the Navy, but did not go into combat; instead, he was stationed in Norfolk, Virginia. So for four years Katherine was essentially a single mother raising two young daughters, although Anne's maternal grandmother did move in to help. Anne describes her grandmother as being "a very warm, wonderful presence in the house."

When the war ended and Howard returned home, he took a job at the post office, and he and Katherine had two more daughters. In this house full of females, there was a strong emphasis placed on creativity, culture, and imagination.

"My mother was extremely loving, extremely devoted, and extremely committed to educating us and giving us every cultural advantage," Anne says. "She read poetry to us, she told us stories, she was very intensely Catholic and took us to church as far back as I can remember. She really devoted a lot of attention to doing projects with us and making scrapbooks with beautiful religious pictures.

"The reading of poetry was a really big thing. We'd gather on her bed, and she'd read to us from a book of poetry by Marjorie Barrows—she'd read our favorite poems over and over again. She wanted us to be very culturally enriched; she wanted us to go to the best schools that she could afford. Of course, she couldn't really afford good schools, so that didn't work out—we went to the parish school. But she was always encouraging us to read and be creative; she was always telling us we could do anything we wanted. She told us marvelous stories about the Brontë sisters and George Eliot and how these women had become famous authors even though some of them had to write under the names of men. She just filled our heads with a sense of freedom and the sense that we could complete our goals."

It's natural to wonder, when hearing about a childhood so rich in storytelling, if that can turn someone into a writer. But of course it's a question that can probably never be answered. Whether writers are born or molded will always be a mystery. But either way, they are influenced.

"I don't know why somebody becomes a writer," Anne says, "but from the earliest times, I certainly wanted to be a writer. And I felt that I could be. I loved hearing about all those writers. She also told us about George Sand. I remember her taking me to see the movie *A Song to Remember,* about Chopin and his love affair with George Sand. I was very infatuated with all of that. She told us over and over again that she wanted to raise four perfectly healthy children and four geniuses. She believed in our creative freedom. We could make color pictures and paste them all over the walls. We could write on the walls; we could do anything we wanted creatively. She also loved taking us to the park. . . .

"She was a very caring mother. She was the type of mother who today would be called a homeschooler, even though we did go to school. But she gave us a more interesting education at home than the education we received at school."

Anne and her sisters went to all-girls Catholic schools, and she credits the nuns with also being very intent on educating the students. "I emerged from my childhood with a strong sense that I could do anything I wanted."

❧❧❧

But as enchanting and creative as the O'Brien home was—as nurturing and supportive as Katherine was— there was a dark undercurrent.

Katherine was an alcoholic, and if alcoholism could be measured by size—like a figure from a child's fairy tale—hers would have blocked out the stars. When she drank, she didn't stop.

"She would drink in spells," Anne says. "And at those times she'd be completely comatose or unconscious for days at a time. She'd get up in the night when we were asleep and find the liquor she'd hidden and then drink until she passed out. So we saw her passed out more than we actually saw her drunk. Then she would recover from these spells, and she'd come back to us and she'd be sparkling and witty and wonderful and beautiful, just as if nothing had happened. But as she got older, the spells became more frequent and more destructive to her health."

Katherine died coming out of one of those spells. She'd been taken to a cousin's house to be "dried out," and she had a seizure. Anne was 14 years old.

"No one knew in those days that you couldn't take a heavy-drinking person like that and just dry them out."

Howard had sent Katherine to their cousin's house for her own safety. She was drinking so heavily that someone had to always be there to watch her and make sure she didn't fall and hurt herself or light a cigarette and burn the house down. One of Anne's sisters was in the hospital, and the family was there caring for her, so there was no one at home to look out for Katherine.

On the morning her mother died, Anne was given the news by her aunt. "I went over to the church and prayed at the altar, and I felt a great sense of release because the suffering was over, but I also felt a kind of terrible shock. It was much worse for my two younger sisters, though. Alice and I had known her during the good years when she always read us poetry and took us to movies and enriched our lives in so many ways. They hadn't been exposed enough to that."

It's hard to figure out how and when to grieve when there's a house to run and young children who need to be cared for. Howard expected Alice and Anne to take on the responsibilities of the household, to fill in the vacuum that Katherine's death had left them with. But Anne had just turned 15, and she didn't want those responsibilities.

"I wanted to go out, to date—I didn't want to stay home and do housework and take care of two small children. I felt angry and resentful at his efforts to try and force me into that role. Especially since he felt that the two youngest should have no responsibilities whatsoever—he felt so sorry for them."

Perhaps out of helplessness and need, Howard remarried about a year and a half after Katherine's death. Ultimately, Anne says, it was not a happy marriage.

Whatever resentments lingered between Anne and her father eventually vanished in the wash of years. When Anne's first book, *Interview with the Vampire,* was published in 1976, she flew to Texas, where Howard was then living, and presented him with the first copy.

He died in New Orleans in 1991 after he fell and broke a hip while visiting Anne. He was hospitalized for two months after his fall, and Anne spent days on end with him. She has felt over the years some guilt that she didn't take on more of the home responsibilities after her mother's death, but that's one of the weights that life hands everyone—looking back at decisions we made in our teens from the vantage point of age and feeling our hearts sink at the memory. What matters, though, is the peace we make with others; Anne and Howard were lucky enough to find that.

✿✿✿

Even though she was so young when her mother died, Anne says, "She was the strongest influence in my life. She was so verbally adroit, so interesting, so rich. She had so many stories to tell. Talking and storytelling in the Irish way was such a part of her—she had a profound influence on me. And she had a great sense of humor. She read us jokes from *Reader's Digest,* and we'd just die laughing."

Katherine died at such a formative point in Anne's life. She never got to see her daughter marry and become a mother herself; she never got to glow with pride over Anne's tremendous success as a writer. But she always lived inside Anne—guiding her and encouraging her. As a mother, she handed down the gift of storytelling, the enchantment of imagination. Even death can't dismantle that.

Marjorie Barrows, one of the poets who influenced Anne as a child, wrote:

A fairy seed I planted,
So dry and white and old,
There sprang a vine enchanted
With magic flowers of gold.

✿✿✿

Katherine Allen O'Brien gave her children the magic of believing that they could achieve anything they wanted. She taught them to plant their dreams and watch them grow. It's a timeless lesson, one that Anne now embodies and passes on to others.

→»-«-

(Alice:) Deborah Feingold; (mother:) Alice Hoffman

Alice [foreground] and her mother, Sherry

aLice Hoffman

Alice Hoffman is the best-selling author of 19 novels, two collections of short stories, and eight books for children and young adults. Her work has been published in more than 20 languages. Several of her books, including *Practical Magic* and *Aquamarine,* have been made into films. Her most recent book is *The Third Angel.*

❄ ❄ ❄

In Alice Hoffman's novel *Seventh Heaven,* Nora Silk—a divorced, single mother—moves into a housing development on Long Island, where it's quite obvious she doesn't fit in. "She was based emotionally on my mother," Alice says. In the novel, the men hungrily steal glances at Nora, while the women dole out harsh judgments:

> The other mothers on the street could see her, up on a stepladder with a rag in her hand. Beside the ladder, her baby played in the dirt and she didn't seem to notice that his socks were black and his hands were caked with mud. The baby put twigs and fallen leaves into his mouth, and all he wore was a light woolen sweater over thin pajamas. The mothers on the block thought they could hear her singing "A Fool Such as I" as she washed her windows. They saw the bottle of Windex in her hand and they noticed that she wore no wedding ring.

"My mother was not like other mothers," Alice says. "But all the things I used to resent her for I admire her for now."

❧❧❧

Sherry Klurfeld was born in 1923 in New York. She met Jerome Hoffman when they were both teenagers and working as counselors at a summer camp. They were in their early 20s when they married. At the start of World War II, Jerome joined the Army and was sent to France.

It wasn't until after the war that the Hoffman family started growing. Sherry had her first child—Alice's older brother—in 1949, at 26. Three years later, she gave birth to Alice.

"We lived on Long Island," Alice says. "We had one of those little, teeny-tiny, ticky-tacky houses for returning GIs that were really cheap. It was kind of like a Levittown."

For the first few years of Alice's life, her father was mostly absent. She does remember him frequently dropping her and her brother off at their grandparents' house . . . but that's a memory about leaving, not staying.

When Alice was eight, she and her brother were told that their parents were going to divorce.

"I remember them calling us in and saying, 'Don't tell anyone, but we're not going to be living together anymore.' I didn't know that was even a possibility. Divorce was very unusual then. When I was growing up,

I didn't meet anyone else whose parents were divorced until I went to college. From the age of eight to when I got to college, I was the only person I knew with divorced parents."

Sherry began a new life as a single mother, which meant that the Hoffmans became the "different" family in the neighborhood.

"It was a blue-collar, working-class neighborhood; and my mother was extremely Bohemian," Alice says. "It was a really bad fit. There were kids who weren't allowed to come play at my house. There were people in town who turned their noses up at us. My mother was just different from all the other mothers. She didn't wear makeup; she listened to the Rolling Stones. She was very anti-authority. On Thanksgiving, she took us to a French restaurant. It was just us and two flight attendants in there. Of course, now I'd love to go to a French restaurant on Thanksgiving. But back then I just wanted a normal life. A normal family. A normal mother. A mother who would bake cookies, who would be there when I got home from school. I wanted Donna Reed."

One reason Sherry was not there when Alice came home from school was that she had to work to support her family . . . yet another factor that set them apart from everyone else in town.

"None of my friends' mothers worked. At first my mother taught nursery school. Then she was a social worker—she worked with unwed mothers, of which there were many back then. She worked in foster care and later in protective services. It was intense, but she was really good at it. She was very nonjudgmental."

One big difference between Sherry and her fictional counterpart Nora Silk was that Nora cleaned the house and kept things reasonably tidy. Sherry Hoffman would never have been spotted on a ladder with a bottle of Windex. In fact . . .

"My mother didn't clean the house for 40 years," Alice says. "Sometimes my grandmother would come over and clean up. Or I did, especially if I had friends coming over. But she just couldn't be bothered. My father had left us with antique furniture, and she completely ruined all of it. The dogs would climb all over the English mahogany tables. It was a wreck."

And then there were the boyfriends—definitely not something Donna Reed would have had.

"She dated. And for many years, she lived with one of her boyfriends, which was just not done at that time. But she honestly didn't care what people thought."

Alice had to fend for herself in a home that had no rules, in a town that sat in judgment of her family. It's not hard to see how a child would need to escape into imaginary realms—realms that would, years later, become an adult's artistry.

❂❂❂

Alice's success as a writer came fairly early; her first novel was published in 1977. But strangely—and for reasons that elude Alice—she and Sherry never discussed her work.

"I didn't include her in that part of my life," Alice admits. "But then, I don't think I even included myself. I was kind of running away from my own life for a while. Yet she was my muse in many ways. She allowed me the freedom of thinking outside the box, and she gave me the sense that I could do whatever I wanted. That's a huge gift. When I told her that I wanted to be a writer, there wasn't anything like, 'But you have to make a living.' She just said, 'Oh, good.' I'm so glad now that she was my mother."

As often happens, when Alice became a mother (she has two sons), it brought her closer to Sherry.

"Having children, you make so many mistakes, and you feel so flawed—it does open you up to your parents to a certain extent. I felt like I was very flawed as a parent, and it made me much more understanding of what my mother had had to go through, especially doing it alone."

Sherry never did remarry, although Jerome did. "The sad thing was, I think because of her marriage, my mother could never seem to choose an equal partner to be with."

When Alice mentions her past resentment toward her mother—"I wish I hadn't been so angry"—she says it with a weight to her voice that suggests she thinks about this often.

The memory of anger is what punishes, especially if the anger was toward parents. Long after the emotion has gone, its vapor trail cuts across the psyche. But it's clear when listening to Alice's recollections that anger never crowded out love and admiration for the times Sherry really shone as a mother.

"My mother always stuck up for me. Whenever I got in trouble in school, she would be ready to fight to the death—*against* them and *for* me. In high school, I was a really bad student. And there was a paper in math class we had to turn in at the end of the term. I knew I couldn't do it, and a girl in my class let me copy hers. I copied it exactly, but she got an *A* and I got a *C*. I was so pissed off that I went up to the teacher and said, 'I copied this, and the other person got an *A*.' He was outraged, he called my mother, we ended up in the principal's office. And my mother said, 'Well, why did she get a *C* when the other person got an *A*?' She couldn't get past the unfair judgment. They were shocked by her reaction. Of course, I did get suspended. But it taught me a lot—she was always on my side."

Over the years, Alice has realized that early on there was a subtle role reversal in the mother/daughter dance. She was the one who wanted an orderly, well-kept home, while Sherry was the one who could never seem to clean her room. That dynamic traveled through the years with them, although they never spoke about it.

"I wish now that I'd lived more in the moment—that I'd been more able to accept her as my friend instead of trying to make her into my mother, because she didn't know how to do that."

❀❀❀

When Sherry began having serious health problems, there was no choice but to put her in a care facility where she could have the constant attention of nurses. But her appetite for life and for fun wasn't diminished by poor health.

"She'd be blaring Howard Stern on the radio," Alice says. "She just got so much enjoyment out of life."

One of the health challenges she faced was breast cancer, which Alice would also go through just as her mother was recovering from the disease. There was a moment when Sherry was being wheeled into surgery that seemed to suggest that she, too, had come to understand the role reversal that had occurred between her and Alice.

"They'd given her some kind of drug," Alice says. "And I was standing there with my husband. The nurse said, 'Say good-bye to your mom'—to me, of course. But my mother said, 'Bye, Mom.' I thought, *Well, that's it in a nutshell.*"

Sherry died in the summer of 1999, just a few days after John F. Kennedy, Jr., died. It was terribly hot that month, Alice remembers . . .

"I was still going through treatment for breast cancer, so I couldn't see my mother as often as I wanted, but we talked several times a day. She talked a lot about John Kennedy, Jr.'s plane going down, and she'd say, 'Why am I still alive and he's dead?' She was kind of obsessed with that. She also told me, which I'm so grateful for, that she had no fear of death."

So is it possible that she was expecting to die?

"No, she was expecting to go to the movies. She and her grandson had plans to go see *Eyes Wide Shut* that day. I think her body just failed her."

Alice came into her house—their summer home on Cape Cod, which is where she was when we spoke—to find a voice mail from her brother telling her their mother had died. At moments like that, the environment becomes complicit; the rooms, the walls, the area rugs suddenly become saturated with sorrow and memories and loss. They can never go back to being just things in a house.

"It's very hard for me to be here now," she tells me, "without thinking of her."

✤✤✤

Alice knows that one of the most important things Sherry left her with was "the sense that I could do anything I wanted to do and be whatever I wanted to be." You can't have a stronger foundation than that—something that becomes clear the longer one lives. Sherry also left her with an appreciation for the art of having fun. "She really had such a good time. I wish I could be more like her now."

But . . . "My biggest regret is that I didn't spend more time with her."

It might be that as her muse, Sherry is always spending time with her daughter—whispering over her shoulder, breathing into stories as Alice is writing them. Storytelling is a mysterious thing. It's woven from experiences, from dreams, from imagination, from glimpsing into other lives and wading through your own. It's also woven from hope—the hope that others will follow you through the garden gate and into another world.

One of Alice's books for young adults is *Green Angel*—a slim, magical little book in which a postapocalyptic tale is told by a 15-year-old girl named Green whose entire family is lost in the disaster. The book ends with these lines:

> I found a ream of white paper in a desk drawer. Then I understood the path my mother had spoken of for me. Every white page looked like a garden, in which anything might grow.
>
> I sat down at the table with the pen and the ink. I spread out the clean, white pages.
>
> Then and there, I began to tell their story.

➤➤➤ ◄◄◄

Kathy [left] with her mother, Lorraine; and sister, Sharon

kathy smith

Kathy Smith has been a leading force in the health and wellness industry since 1980, having sold more than 16 million workout videos worldwide. She's written several best-selling books, including *Feed Muscle Shrink Fat*. Her recent projects include a series of fitness segments on *Health Corner* with Leeza Gibbons on Lifetime and a nutrition and exercise initiative targeting type 2 diabetes.

❀ ❀ ❀

Kathy Smith wears a diamond ring that was once her mother's. It was the only thing salvaged from the fiery plane crash in which her mother died. Years ago the diamond started to come loose in its setting, and Kathy put the ring in her jewelry box, planning to have it reset but not quite getting around to it. When a friend urged her to go see a much-touted medium, she went even though she wasn't sure she believed in such things.

"Your mother is here with us," the medium told her. "She wants you to start wearing her ring again. It's the one thing connecting you."

Kathy had the ring reset, and now she doesn't take it off.

Diamonds come from deep inside the earth; they spew out in volcanoes, in eruptions of extraordinary temperatures. They survive the flames. So do hearts, but it takes a while to realize that.

❂❂❂

Lorraine Gautsch was born in La Crosse, Wisconsin, in 1928 to German parents. She met Carl Stefferud when she was 16 and he was 17; two years later, at 18, she married him. He joined the military as an Air Force pilot, and Lorraine became an officer's wife. She had her first daughter, Sharon, in 1949; three years later, Kathy was born.

"I was a military brat," Kathy says, laughing at the now-familiar term. "My father was stationed all around the world. We were in São Paulo, Brazil; we were in Mobile, Alabama; we were in Texas, Hawaii, Illinois. I was raised in a very disciplined house—we were trained to answer the phone: "Stefferud residence." Our life was the Officers' Club and dressing properly to go there.

"We lived on military bases most of the time, but as we traveled around, we sometimes lived off base in small houses. You get really used to Dad going off to work every day in his uniform. My mother's life as a military wife was about protocol, receptions, conformity. Everyone's home kind of looked the same, and the uniforms looked the same except for the number of bars each man wore."

Growing up, Kathy never spent more than three years in one place. Intuitively, children who grow up like that learn to protect their feelings by not getting too attached to anyone—they know that another good-bye, another move, is just around the corner. The cords that bind are kept thin, easy to snap. It's too costly emotionally to weave strong ropes between you and the people you're going to have to leave. It's something that Kathy knows has followed her throughout her life.

"I don't really know who my tribe is," she says. "I've fit into different circles of friends at different times. But I've never been sure who my tribe is."

Children are resilient. Even in a life where putting down roots is a temporary exercise, they will extract things that feel dependable. Lorraine worked hard to create a grounded, dependable home environment for her daughters.

"What I loved so much about my mother," Kathy says, "is that there was a routine. When you live on bases, you go shopping at the commissaries and the PXs, and you get everything at a discount because you're shopping on base. She would take us with her, and we would be wearing the cutest little dresses—my sister and I always matched; we always had our hair curled because little girls weren't supposed to have straight hair. At Easter we'd wear bonnets. We always had dinner at 5:30 when Dad came home. My job was to help my mom fix the salad; Sharon's job was to help with some other part of the meal. My mother was very traditional, and there was a real sense of order and security in that."

❂ ❂ ❂

But beneath the surface, things were less grounded. One of the daily routines of life on the military bases was cocktail hour—a harmless enough thing if only a moderate amount of alcohol is consumed. But Lorraine's drinking, her daughters came to notice, was not exactly moderate.

"It was very common for my parents to have a Manhattan or a martini at 5:00 or 5:30. Everyone did it. No one thought anything about it—it was just what everyone did. But when I got into high school, I started noticing this pattern with my mother: Monday, there would be a little drinking, but she'd still be a wonderful mom; Tuesday she'd still be sort of okay; on Wednesday she'd be drinking more. The cycle would build through the week until she started getting abusive to my dad, and by the end of the week, there would be some blowup fight. Sharon and I would go to our rooms, and we'd hear them fighting at night. It was very uncomfortable."

Even though alcoholism at that time wasn't as widely acknowledged or discussed as it is now, it's possible that Carl might have been able to get Lorraine some help. But he would never get that chance.

When Kathy was in her last two years of high school, the family was stationed in Belleville, Illinois. Three days before her graduation, Carl had a heart attack and died.

"He was at the office, standing up to give a debriefing, and because he had a very good sense of humor, everybody thought he was joking when he fell down. When they realized he wasn't, they rushed him to the emergency room. He'd had a massive heart attack. . . ."

Carl was 42 years old.

At 41, Lorraine was suddenly and unexpectedly a widow. Anyone in that situation would run into the comforting arms of a friend. Unfortunately for Lorraine, that friend was liquor.

"The drinking wasn't so bad that she wasn't functional," Kathy recalls. "But I remember coming home some evenings and finding her sitting in a dark room in this wooden rocking chair we had then. She'd have Tom Jones records on—she loved Tom Jones. So there she'd be, with "What's New Pussycat?" playing on the stereo, and she'd be rocking back and forth with a drink in her hand in this dark room. There was such an aura of sadness around her. . . . I felt so sorry for her. And I was aware at that point of a shift in our relationship, how in some ways, *I* became the mother."

She stayed at home with Lorraine for a while, choosing to go to college in Illinois. She was the only daughter at home—Sharon was at college in Hawaii. But after about a year, Kathy also decided to go to Hawaii, along with a couple of girlfriends. They planned to drive cross-country to California, put their cars on a boat to Hawaii, and fly over themselves. Saying good-bye to her mother the day Kathy left is a memory that still brings up tears. . . .

"I have this vivid image of standing there hugging my mother and both of us crying so hard, holding on to each other so tightly. On the one hand, I was glad to get out of there because of the situation, but I felt so sorry for her, and I felt so alone. I was losing such a part of me—I was losing this good part of me when I took off."

Left alone, Lorraine decided to go back to Wisconsin, and while she was there, she met a man named David Brown who flew private planes. They hadn't known each other for too long before getting married. Kathy and Sharon flew from Hawaii to Wisconsin for the wedding, which Kathy admits was a bit strange. But, she says, "We were happy for her."

A few months later, on a winter day, Lorraine and David were returning to Wisconsin from Illinois on one of his planes. That particular plane had pontoons on it for landing on water. With the freezing temperatures, he should have removed them but had neglected to do so. They iced up and the plane went down in a farmer's field, flipped over, and burst into flames.

"My aunt called me—I was in Hawaii—and I remember screaming into the phone, 'Why is this happening to us?!' It had only been two years since my dad died. Then I ran outside and sat on the curb crying hysterically. I remember thinking, *Why plan for the future when it can end just like that, so suddenly?*"

It was 1971. Kathy was 19 years old. America was in a state of revolution on many fronts—the Vietnam War, the sexual revolution, women's lib, drugs. People her age were gleefully running from their parents to start adventurous lives on their own. And she was sitting on a curb weeping, having just been orphaned, feeling completely and utterly alone.

"Something like that really shapes you," she says. "And in many ways it shaped my success. Because you do one of two things—you either go under or you find a way to succeed."

❀❀❀

It's strange how life turns us onto the path we're meant to be on. Weighed down with grief, splintery with anxiety, Kathy began accompanying her then-boyfriend, a football player, on his daily runs.

"I just started sprinting a quarter mile one day, then a half mile, then a mile. And I'd come back from the runs and feel so much better. The depression, the sadness, the confusion had lifted. That's when I started to make the connection between exercise and emotions. I went from being kind of comatose to feeling that I could go on and I'd be okay.

"When I started running, it was just at the time that Ken Cooper had coined the term *aerobics,* which means 'with oxygen.' And he was showing how heart patients could benefit from running. Back then, if you were a heart patient, you weren't supposed to have sex, you weren't supposed to climb stairs, you weren't supposed to exert yourself. And there was a doctor in Hawaii who met at a park with 56 heart patients—his goal was to get them ready to run a marathon. So, I would go and listen to his lectures and train, and I ran my first marathon in 1975."

While the other runners were healing their physically damaged hearts, Kathy was healing a heart that had been drowning in grief.

"That was the beginning for me of understanding that what you put in your body, how you move your body, affects your mind. It lifted me out of my confusion and depression—it's what saved my life."

❂❂❂

Kathy found her career—her path in life—through discipline and strength. Strength is something she now realizes Lorraine had during all those years of moving constantly, of living on military bases and being an officer's wife.

"My mother was the one who had to run everything," Kathy says. "My dad would take off and go on his fun adventures, go off on his planes—there was something kind of romantic about all that. But she had to run the household, take care of the moving every few years. The lack of roots affected her, too—she didn't have a stable home environment. She'd have to pack up the house, sell things, move us, sometimes to another country. And, also, as a military wife, she had to present a proper image; that's very important in that world."

Kathy is now a mother of two girls. "When I had my daughters—they're now 19 and 17—I really started to appreciate my mom and miss her and wish that she were around. Especially when my kids were young, one and two years old, I wished I could call her and ask her questions."

❂❂❂

From the flames that engulfed a small plane on an icy winter day and took two lives—flames that left almost nothing intact or recognizable—a diamond was recovered. Stronger than the flames, it's worn by the other survivor who had to search a while to find her strength. She found it in running; in asking her heart to work harder, grow larger, pump more blood. She found it in the mystery and the questions about why she was left so alone at such a young age, because drifting between the questions was a feeling that she *wasn't* alone. She trusted that feeling and kept running forward. It's what runners do—they look for roads, trails, paths . . . and if they can't find them, they make them.

→≫≪←

acknowledgments

hank you to all the women who so graciously gave their time and trusted me with their stories. Thank you also to Jill Kramer, Christy Salinas, Alex Freemon, and everyone else at Hay House; and to Jim Nagle for making the introduction.

⟶»«⟵

We hope you enjoyed this Hay House book. If you'd like to receive a free catalog featuring additional Hay House books and products, or if you'd like information about the Hay Foundation, please contact:

Hay House, Inc.
P.O. Box 5100
Carlsbad, CA 92018-5100

(760) 431-7695 or **(800) 654-5126**
(760) 431-6948 (fax) or **(800) 650-5115 (fax)**
www.hayhouse.com® • **www.hayfoundation.org**

☻ ☻ ☻

Published and distributed in Australia by:
Hay House Australia Pty. Ltd., 18/36 Ralph St., Alexandria NSW 2015
Phone: 612-9669-4299 • *Fax:* 612-9669-4144
www.hayhouse.com.au

Published and distributed in the United Kingdom by:
Hay House UK, Ltd., 292B Kensal Rd., London W10 5BE
Phone: 44-20-8962-1230 • *Fax:* 44-20-8962-1239
www.hayhouse.co.uk

Published and distributed in the Republic of South Africa by:
Hay House SA (Pty), Ltd., P.O. Box 990, Witkoppen 2068
Phone/Fax: 27-11-467-8904 • orders@psdprom.co.za
www.hayhouse.co.za

Published in India by: Hay House Publishers India,
Muskaan Complex, Plot No. 3, B-2, Vasant Kunj, New Delhi 110 070
Phone: 91-11-4176-1620 • *Fax:* 91-11-4176-1630 • www.hayhouse.co.in

Distributed in Canada by:
Raincoast, 9050 Shaughnessy St., Vancouver, B.C. V6P 6E5
Phone: (604) 323-7100 • *Fax:* (604) 323-2600 • www.raincoast.com

☻ ☻ ☻

Tune in to **HayHouseRadio.com®** for the best in inspirational talk radio featuring top Hay House authors! And, sign up via the Hay House USA Website to receive the Hay House online newsletter and stay informed about what's going on with your favorite authors. You'll receive bimonthly announcements about Discounts and Offers, Special Events, Product Highlights, Free Excerpts, Giveaways, and more!
www.hayhouse.com®